HOUSING ISSUES, LAWS AND PROGRAMS

UNUSED FEDERAL PROPERTY FOR HOMELESS ASSISTANCE

AN EXAMINATION

Housing Issues, Laws and Programs

Additional books in this series can be found on Nova's website under the Series tab.

Additional e-books in this series can be found on Nova's website under the e-book tab.

HOUSING ISSUES, LAWS AND PROGRAMS

UNUSED FEDERAL PROPERTY FOR HOMELESS ASSISTANCE

AN EXAMINATION

JULIA L. BROWN
EDITOR

nova publishers
New York

Library of Congress Cataloging-in-Publication Data

ISBN: 978-1-63482-995-3

Published by Nova Science Publishers, Inc. † New York

CONTENTS

PREFACE

The federal government holds thousands of properties that agencies no longer need to accomplish their missions. When the government disposes of unneeded properties—through transfer, donation, or sale—it generates savings by eliminating maintenance costs. In addition, when state or local governments, nonprofits, or businesses acquire unneeded federal properties, they may be used to provide services to the public, such as temporary housing, or contribute to economic development. Title V of the McKinney-Vento Homeless Assistance Act enacted in 1987 created a program to assist the homeless, in part, by identifying unused federal real property and making it available to homeless assistance providers. This book examines the identification and transfer of federal real property to homeless assistance providers; and the benefits and challenges homeless assistance providers and national advocacy organizations reported in identifying, acquiring, and using federal real property, and the potential actions that could help to address these challenges. This book also provides an explanation of the central role played by the General Services Administration (GSA) in the disposal of federal real property at most agencies. It then provides a discussion of the unique disposal processes at DOD and the U.S. Postal Service (USPS), which each have independent statutory authority to dispose of their own properties. It concludes with an overview of the environmental and historic preservation requirements that apply to the disposal of properties at all federal agencies.

In: Unused Federal Property ...
Editor: Julia L. Brown

ISBN: 978-1-63482-995-3

Chapter 1

FEDERAL REAL PROPERTY: MORE USEFUL INFORMATION TO PROVIDERS COULD IMPROVE THE HOMELESS ASSISTANCE PROGRAM*

United States Government Accountability Office

WHY GAO DID THIS STUDY

Title V of the McKinney-Vento Homeless Assistance Act enacted in 1987 created a program to assist the homeless, in part, by identifying unused federal real property and making it available to homeless assistance providers.

GAO was asked to review the implementation of Title V of the McKinney-Vento Homeless Assistance Act. This report examines: (1) the identification and transfer of federal real property to homeless assistance providers and (2) the benefits and challenges homeless assistance providers and national advocacy organizations reported in identifying, acquiring, and using federal real property, and the potential actions that could help to address these challenges. GAO obtained information and data from HUD and the Department of Health and Human Services (HHS) on the properties reported since the program's inception and interviewed officials from GSA, HHS, and HUD. GAO also obtained views on the program from officials at (1) nine

* This is an edited, reformatted and augmented version of the United States Government Accountability Office publication, GAO-14-739, dated September 2014.

federal agencies, representing a range of size in their real property portfolios; (2) eleven homeless assistance providers (including eight that received property), representing a range of locations, size of property, and services provided; and (3) national homeless-advocacy organizations.

What GAO Recommends

Congress should consider changing (1) the scope of properties to be reported to HUD with respect to the types of properties that may be less likely to be useful to assist the homeless and (2) the frequency of *Federal Register* reporting.

What GAO Found

Since inception in 1987, the nationwide Title V homeless-assistance program has transferred 122 properties from federal agencies to homeless assistance providers. Of these properties, 81 are currently being used to provide a range of homeless assistance services nationwide. Such services include transitional housing, referral services, and emergency shelter. However, few of the properties that the Department of Housing and Urban Development (HUD) has listed as suitable and available since the program's inception received applications from homeless assistance providers. In most cases, the properties may not have actually been practical for homeless service providers to use. For example, in 2013 about 80 percent of these properties were for off-site use only—meaning that a provider would need to physically move the property in order to use it. HUD officials told us that they would prefer that agencies not be required to report certain types of properties at all, such as those for off-site use only. The current statutory requirement for agencies to report all properties that fall within four broad categories—excess, surplus, underutilized, and unutilized— may not be effective for certain types of properties. Such exclusion could allow HUD officials to focus on the suitable and available properties that may be more likely to assist the homeless.

Of the 11 homeless assistance providers we interviewed, the eight case study providers that acquired property cited benefits from the Title V homeless assistance program, such as expanding services and obtaining real property at no cost. These benefits notwithstanding, the providers identified challenges, such as identifying available properties. These findings are consistent with reports from national homeless advocacy organizations. HUD reports properties in the *Federal Register* multiple times a year as required. The United States Interagency Council on Homelessness (USICH), which plays a coordination role, provides a link on its website to the HUD reports. Nonetheless, according to national homeless advocates, many homeless assistance providers remain unaware of the availability of properties because the *Federal Register* is not user-friendly. Further, HUD lists many of the same properties more than once in the *Federal Register*, as required, even though they may not be useful to homeless assistance providers. In the past, some in Congress and the executive branch have raised issues about reporting requirements; the basic issue has been that some requirements result in reports that may be burdensome to produce, or not very useful. Modifying reporting requirements to reduce the frequency of reporting related to properties that are less likely to be useful to homeless providers could help, while also allowing HUD to continue to fulfill its responsibilities.

ABBREVIATIONS

ARCH	A Regional Coalition for Housing
BRAC	Base Realignment and Closure Act
DOD	Department of Defense
DOE	Department of Energy
DOI	Department of the Interior
EPA	Environmental Protection Agency
GSA	General Services Administration
HHS	Department of Health and Human Services
HUD	Department of Housing and Urban Development
LRA	local redevelopment authority
OMB	Office of Management and Budget
NLEC	New Life Evangelistic Center
OneCPD	Community Planning and Development Web site
USICH	U.S. Interagency Council on Homelessness
VA	Department of Veterans Affairs
VOALA	Volunteers of America of Los Angeles

September 30, 2014

The Honorable Thomas R. Carper
Chairman
The Honorable Tom Coburn,
M.D. Ranking Member
Committee on Homeland Security and Governmental Affairs
United States Senate

Estimates of the homeless population in the United States vary widely. According to the Department of Housing and Urban Development (HUD) 610,042 people in the United States were homeless on a single night in January 2013, and more than a third of these people were living in unsheltered locations, such as under bridges, in cars, or in abandoned buildings.[1] According to the National Law Center on Homelessness and Poverty, the numbers of Americans experiencing homelessness is estimated between 1.5 million to 3.5 million in a given year.[2] At the same time, we have previously reported that federal agencies continue to hold thousands of unneeded and underutilized properties that annually cost the government over a billion dollars to operate.[3] As a result of this and other long-standing problems, we have designated federal real property as a high-risk area.[4] Title V of the McKinney-Vento Homeless Assistance Act (the Act), as amended, created a program to assist the homeless, in part, by using public resources and programs—including unused federal real property—in a more coordinated manner to meet the needs of homeless Americans.[5]

In general, Title V of the Act requires federal landholding agencies to identify and make available for homeless assistance real property under their control that they are not fully utilizing or no longer need before properties are disposed through other means. If a property is published by HUD as suitable and available, eligible applicants, such as homeless assistance providers and local governments, may apply to obtain the real property at no cost for the provision of a broad range of services for the homeless, including shelter, job training, and storage.

However, implementing the Title V homeless assistance program requirements has presented challenges. Our prior work has found that legal and budgetary challenges continue to hamper agencies' disposal efforts. Since much of the unneeded federal real property may have no remaining useful life, may require extensive environmental remediation, may be located within secure compounds, or require off-site removal, it, for example, may not be useful to assist the homeless.[6] You asked us to determine how this program is performing both in terms of government operations and for homeless assistance providers. This report addresses two objectives:

1. The identification and transfer of federal real properties for homeless assistance under the Title V homeless assistance program.
2. The benefits and challenges homeless assistance providers and national advocacy organizations reported in identifying, acquiring, and using federal real property, and potential actions that could help address these challenges.

To determine what is known about the identification and transfer of federal real properties for homeless assistance under Title V, we reviewed the requirements of Title V of the Act as they apply to the General Services Administration (GSA), the Department of Health and Human Services (HHS), HUD, and the U.S. Interagency Council on Homelessness (USICH). We obtained estimates from HUD of the number of underutilized, unutilized, excess, and surplus properties reported by landholding agencies and the number that HUD determined to be suitable and published as available for homeless use since the program's inception in 1987 through March 31, 2014—the date of the most recently available information. To assess the reliability of these estimates, we interviewed officials from HUD about how the estimates were derived and determined that the information provided by the agency provides a reasonable basis, with caveats, for reporting the number of properties that have been screened and found suitable and available. In addition, to determine the types of properties reported, we analyzed HUD's annual reports of suitable/available and suitable/unavailable properties for years 2008 through 2013. This time frame was selected to include the 5 years prior to this audit. When HUD's annual report for 2013 became available, we added it to the analysis to include the most recent information. From HHS, we also obtained documents and data on the number of notices of interest and applications it received for properties made available for homeless assistance from the program's inception in 1987 through March 31, 2014. To assess the reliability of these data, we interviewed officials from HHS about how the data are collected and maintained, and the importance to the agency of ensuring the completeness of this data, and we determined that the data were sufficiently reliable for the purposes of our report. To understand how federal landholding agencies identify and report real property to HUD pursuant to the Act's requirements, we selected nine landholding agencies to include a range of size among real property portfolios of land and buildings, including GSA, HHS, the three Department of Defense service branches—the U.S. Army, U.S. Air Force, and U.S. Navy—the Department of Energy (DOE), the Department of the Interior (DOI) and the Department of Veterans Affairs (VA),[7] and the Environmental Protection Agency (EPA).[8] We interviewed agency officials from GSA, HHS, HUD, and USICH to understand how they process properties reported under Title V homeless assistance program requirements. We also interviewed agency officials from the nine landholding agencies to obtain their views on how they meet the Act's requirements and their impact on each agency's disposal process. To determine the benefits and challenges that homeless assistance providers and national advocacy organizations report in identifying, acquiring, and using federal real property and potential actions that could help address those challenges, we selected eight homeless assistance organizations that acquired federal real property under the program based on criteria such as the size of the real property acquired under the program, the services provided, geographic distribution, range of experiences, and suggestions from agencies and homeless advocacy organizations. We interviewed representatives from each of the selected organizations, reviewed documentation, and conducted site visits to two properties transferred under the Title V homeless assistance program. We also convened a virtual discussion panel comprised of representatives from three homeless assistance organizations whose applications for federal real property were not approved and interviewed representatives from two national homelessness-advocacy organizations (see app. 1 for more information on our scope and methodology).[9] We conducted this performance audit from September 2013 to September 2014 in accordance with generally accepted government auditing standards. Those standards require that we plan and perform the audit to obtain sufficient, appropriate evidence to provide a reasonable basis for our findings and conclusions based on our audit objectives. We believe that the evidence obtained provides a reasonable basis for our findings and conclusions based on our audit objectives.

BACKGROUND

The McKinney-Vento Homeless Assistance Act created over a dozen programs intended to comprehensively address the needs of homeless Americans. Among these, the Title V homeless assistance program requires federal landholding agencies to make available real property that they identify as excess, surplus, unutilized, or underutilized for possible use to assist the homeless. Title V of the Act designated GSA, HHS, and HUD to administer the program. In addition, Title II of the Act created what is now known as USICH, an independent establishment within the Executive Branch whose mission is to coordinate the federal response to homelessness. The mission of USICH is to create a national partnership to act as a coordinating body between the federal government and the private sector to end homelessness nationally. Title V specifies a number of steps that federal landholding agencies, the three federal agency administrators of the program, and USICH must take to make federal real property—including land and buildings, or both—available for homeless assistance. Figure 1 summarizes key steps in the process and the time frames required to perform those steps.

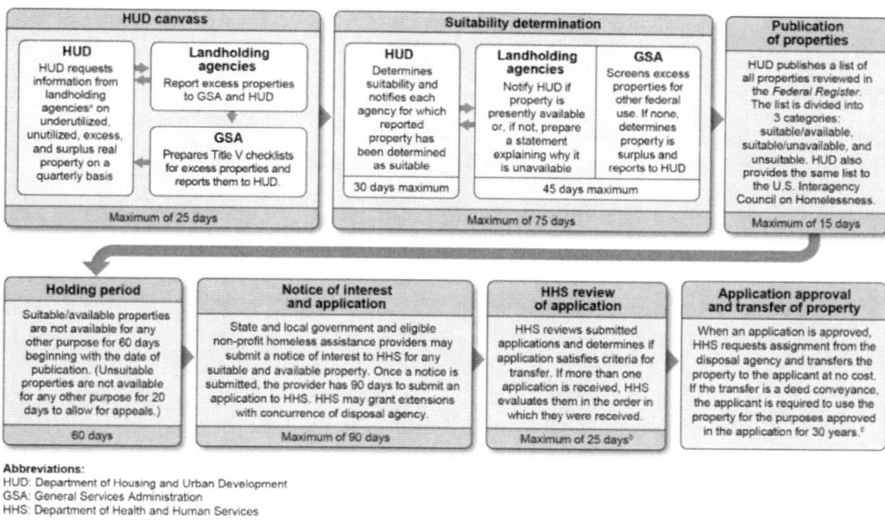

Source: GAO analysis of HUD, GSA, and HHS information. |GAO-14-739.

[a] Some agencies (e.g. DOI and the U.S. Navy) submit Title V checklists on an ongoing basis during the interim between the quarterly canvasses.

[b] HHS has a maximum of 25 days from the date a completed application is received to evaluate the application.

[c] HHS has a process by which the approved program of use may be changed as needed.

Figure 1. The Title V Homeless Assistance Program Process.

Table 1. Categories of Real Property That Landholding Agencies Must Report to the Department of Housing and Urban Development (HUD)

Property category	Description	Where defined
Excess property	Property that an agency has determined is not required to meet the agency's needs or responsibilities.	42 U.S.C. § 1411(i)(2) which incorporates by reference 40 U.S.C. § 102(3).
Surplus property	An excess property that GSA has determined is not required to meet the needs or responsibilities of all federal agencies.	42 U.S.C. § 11411(i)(2) which incorporates by reference 40 U.S.C. § 102(10).
Underutilized property	Property used only irregularly, intermittently, or partially for current agency mission needs.	Implementing regulations promulgated by HUD, GSA, and HHS (24 C.F.R. § 581.1; 45 C.F.R. § 12a.1; 41 C.F.R. § 102-75.1160).
Unutilized property	Property not occupied for current program purposes.	Implementing regulations promulgated by HUD, GSA, and HHS (24 C.F.R. § 581.1; 45 C.F.R. § 12a.1; 41 C.F.R. § 102-75.1160).

Source: GAO analysis. | GAO-14-739.

***HUD canvass*:** HUD surveys the landholding agencies that must identify and report to HUD on a quarterly basis real property that is excess, surplus, underutilized, or unutilized (see table 1).[10]

Once landholding agencies (currently 25 in total) receive HUD's quarterly canvassing letter, they have 25 days to respond. To collect such information, HUD asks landholding agencies to complete a "Title V checklist" for each of the excess, surplus, underutilized, or unutilized properties that they have identified and are required to report.[11] The checklist is a HUD document that requires the landholding agency to provide a variety of summary information about the real property, including its utilization status, accessibility (e.g., in a remote location or behind a secure perimeter), environmental condition, agency contacts, and other information (see app. II for an example of this checklist).

Suitability determination: HUD assigns each reported real property a unique identification number and enters the checklist information into an electronic database. Based on the checklist, HUD must determine the suitability of each real property for homeless assistance. According to implementing regulations, all real property—land, buildings, or both—are suitable unless a property's characteristics include one or more of the following conditions:

- national security concerns, meaning a property is located in an area where the general public is denied access in the interest of national security;
- flammable or explosive materials within 2000 feet of the property;
- located in an airport runway clear zone or military airfield clear zone;
- located in a floodway;
- documented deficiencies, meaning a property with a documented and extensive condition(s) that represents a clear threat to personal physical safety, including structural damage or certain types of environmental contamination; or
- inaccessible, meaning a property is not accessible by road.[12]

After HUD makes a suitability determination, it is to provide this information to the reporting landholding agencies for review, as well as for the *Federal Register* listing that briefly describes the property's condition and status (e.g., underutilized, unutilized, excess, or surplus).[13] Landholding agencies then have 45 days to make any edits, as noted in figure 1, such as changes in the property's status. In addition, landholding agencies must transmit to HUD a statement of the availability of real property, declaring for example that a property is available for homeless assistance or explaining why a property cannot be made available for homeless assistance, such as in the case of a further compelling federal need for the property.

HUD also communicates with GSA, the federal government's real-property disposal agent, to identify excess real properties that landholding agencies have reported to GSA for disposal. If, however, a landholding agency reports real property to GSA that has not been submitted to HUD for a Title V suitability determination, GSA is required to create a Title V checklist and forward it to HUD.[14]

Publication of properties and holding period: Title V requires HUD to publish in the *Federal Register* all properties it reviewed. HUD's *Federal Register* listings typically classify these properties as: 1) suitable and available for homeless assistance; 2) suitable but unavailable for homeless assistance; or 3) unsuitable for homeless assistance. Once published, homeless assistance providers—including state and local governments or eligible private non-profit organizations[15]—have 60 days to submit a "notice of interest" for suitable and available properties, and then 90 days from the date of the "notice of interest," to submit an application to HHS.[16] The real property is not available for any other purpose during the 60-day or 90-day period or during the period in which HHS reviews the application. Interested parties also have 20 days to challenge the suitability determination of real property HUD found unsuitable for homeless assistance. If a notice of interest is not filed for a suitable and available real property within 60 days of its listing in the *Federal Register*, the disposal agency may then proceed with its routine disposal process, in accordance with applicable law.

In addition to publication in the *Federal Register*, the requirements of Title V require GSA, HHS, and HUD to make such efforts as are necessary to ensure the widest possible dissemination of the listing information of available properties. For example, HUD is required to forward lists of all real property published in the *Federal Register* to USICH, which then must distribute relevant portions of the list to state and regional homeless coordinators. Also, when HUD determines an excess real property is suitable and publishes it in the *Federal Register* as available, the implementing regulations require GSA to concurrently notify HHS, HUD, and state and local governments, in addition to homeless assistance providers that have expressed interest in the particular real property, and other organizations, as appropriate, concerning suitable properties.[17]

Notices of interest and application: HHS is to evaluate applications of homeless assistance providers on a first-come, first-serve basis using five criteria defined in HHS implementing regulations.[18] HHS may specify additional criteria for the application package for a given real property if it deems it necessary. The criteria are as follows:

- *Proposed service offering*: the extent and range of proposed services, such as meal, shelter, job training, and counseling.
- *Need*: the demand for the program and the degree to which the available real property will be fully utilized.
- *Implementation time*: the amount of time necessary for the proposed program to become operational.
- *Experience*: demonstrated prior success in operating similar programs and attestations by federal, state and local authorities.

- *Financial ability*: the adequacy of funding that will likely be available to fully run the proposed program and operate the facility.

HHS review of application, application approval, and transfer of property: HHS is to review applications for completeness and, in some cases, may request additional information from the applicant, as necessary. Evaluations must be completed in 25 days from the receipt of the completed application.

If HHS approves an application for underutilized or unutilized real property, the landholding agency can execute a lease of the property to the applicant. In the case of surplus real property, the disposal agency "assigns" the property to HHS, which then becomes the sponsoring agency and transfers the deed to the applicant. Grantees of federal properties under the Title V homeless assistance program must utilize the property in accordance with the approved application for the length of the lease or, in the case of deed conveyances, for 30 years.

Pursuant to HHS policies and procedures, HHS is to perform compliance oversight and ensure that the grantee uses the real property according to the terms in the approved application. To accomplish this, grantees are required to submit annual utilization reports to HHS, and HHS is to conduct site visits of the properties at least once every 5 years. In the event that a grantee is not implementing or is unable to implement the program consistent with the approved application, the property title may revert back to the federal government.[19]

Title V of the Act has been amended several times, including by the Base Closure Community Redevelopment and Homeless Assistance Act of 1994[20] (the Redevelopment Act or Act). According to HUD, this Act aimed to improve the process for disposing buildings and property at military installations under the existing base closure laws. Under the Act, which became effective shortly after the beginning of fiscal year 1995, Department of Defense (DOD) properties disposed under the Defense Base Closure and Realignment Act of 1990[21] were no longer subject to the Title V homeless assistance program requirements. According to HUD, many individuals involved in military base reuse concluded that Title V did not adequately address the multiple interests related to large parcels of surplus federal properties such as military bases. In general, with respect to the disposal of buildings and property located at installations approved for closure or realignment, the Redevelopment Act substituted a community-based process for the Title V homeless assistance program, in which the local redevelopment authority prepares a reuse plan after consulting with representatives of the homeless and other community groups affected by the base closure, and HUD ensures that the plan appropriately balances the needs of the community for economic and other development with the needs of the homeless.[22] We excluded from this report facilities on military bases closed after 1994 and subject to the provisions of the Redevelopment Act, as we are reviewing implementations of the Act's provisions separately and plan to report on the results in 2015.

Several court orders resulting from a 1988 lawsuit filed by the National Law Center on Homelessness and Poverty (National Law Center) and other advocates for the homeless have also shaped the implementation requirements of the Title V homeless assistance program. The 1988lawsuit alleged, and the court found, that the federal government was not fully complying with some Title V requirements. The court issued an order in 1993 imposing requirements beyond those mandated by the statute and implementing regulations, such as more comprehensive reporting requirements and expanded outreach. Unlike the 1993 District Court order, a more recent 2013 order does not require widespread changes to operational administration of the Title V homeless assistance program but rather seeks to better educate the landholding agencies about canvassing their real property and improving the quality of data reported by these agencies for Title V requirements and the Federal Real Property Profile.[23]

122 Properties Transferred Have Provided a Range of Homeless Assistance Services, but Many Properties Reported and Deemed Suitable for Homeless Assistance May Not Be Useful for That Purpose

Under the Title V homeless assistance program, providers have used over 100 transferred properties since program inception through March 31, 2014, to deliver a range of services across the country. However, few of the properties that HUD has determined to be suitable and were available for homeless assistance since the program's inception received applications from homeless assistance service providers. In most cases, properties screened and determined as suitable and available may not have actually been practical for homeless service providers to use. For example, our analysis of HUD's annual reports from 2008 through 2013 found most of the properties published as suitable and available were for off-site use only—meaning that a provider would need to physically move the property in order to use it.

Homeless Assistance Providers Currently Use 81 Title V Properties for a Range of Services across the Country

The Title V homeless assistance program has provided properties with useful facilities. As of March 2014, of the 122 properties transferred since the program's inception in 1987, 81 properties are currently in use by providers. For the other 41 properties, there are several explanations as to why they are no longer in use for homeless assistance. For example, leases for 9 properties were rescinded for failure to use the properties for the agreed upon purposes, and deeds for 8 properties reverted to the government for reasons such as non-compliance or by request of the grantee. Across the country homeless assistance providers use the 81 properties to provide a range of homeless assistance services, such as supportive services, referral services, various forms of temporary or more permanent housing, administrative offices, and clothing or food distribution. The 81 active properties include approximately 470 buildings of about 1.5-million square feet and over 500 acres of land. The properties include a variety of facilities ranging in size from 1900 square feet to 512,000 square feet and vacant land ranging from almost two tenths of an acre to over 96 acres. Of the 81 currently active properties, not-for-profit organizations—such as the Salvation Army, Samaritan House, and Volunteers of America—acquired 69, and local governments acquired 12. A few local governments formed public/not-for-profit collaborations to develop the properties. Figure 2 shows the geographic distribution of the properties.

Providers at 60 of the 81 currently active properties offer multiple services to homeless individuals. For example, one provider said it offers support services such as substance abuse counseling, mental health services, case management, job training and placement. Another provides emergency, transitional, and permanent supportive housing; a health clinic; and daycare services. A third uses a former army depot to distribute goods and clothing (see table 2 for more information on the types of services provided and app. IV for more information on the services provided at each of the 81 locations). According to the National Law Center's 2011 estimate,[24] more than 2.4 million homeless Americans each year have received assistance through the Title V homeless assistance program since its inception.

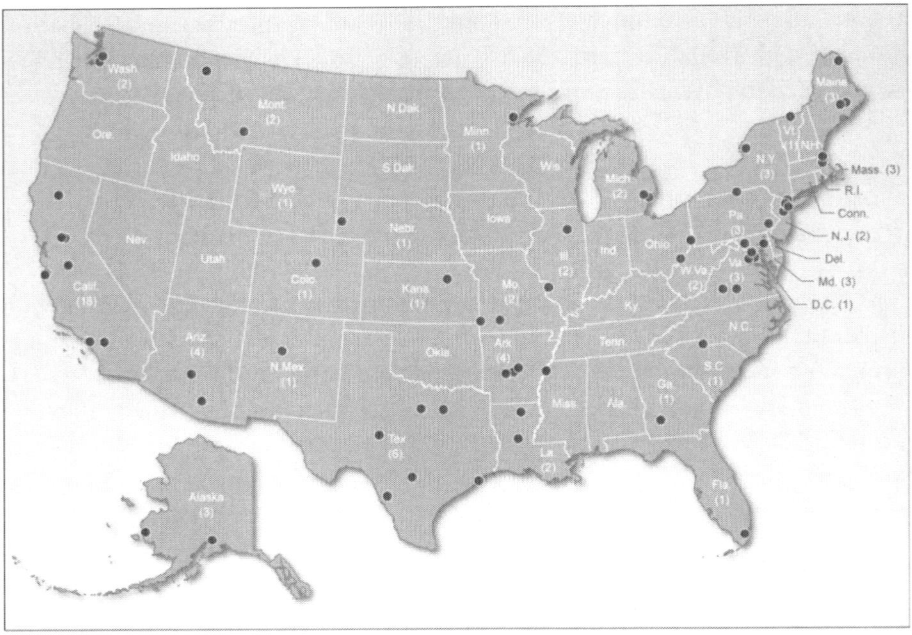

Source: GAO analysis of HHS data. | GAO-14-739.

Note: Circles represent the geographical location of Title V homeless assistance program properties. There may be more than one Title V homeless assistance program real property at a given location. For example, seven Title V homeless-assistance program properties are located at Fort Ord in Monterey, California.

Figure 2. Geographic Distribution of 81 Currently Active Properties as of March 31, 2014.

Table 2. Types of Homeless Assistance Services Offered at the 81 Active Properties, as of March 31, 2014

Services offered[a]	Number of providers offering services
Supportive services[b]	43
Transitional housing[c]	42
Referral services	37
Emergency shelter[d]	19
Permanent supportive housing[e]	12

Services offered[a]	Number of providers offering services
Administrative offices	11
Goods/clothing distribution	8
Education/job training	6
Daycare/day center	5
Food distribution	2
Mental Health	2
Warehouse and storage	2
Case management	1

Source: GAO analysis of HHS information. | GAO-14-739.

[a] Many service providers offer multiple services at the same location based on HHS data. For example, 26 of the 81 service providers offer three different types of services.

[b] Supportive services is a broad category that may include services such as child care; employment assistance; employment counseling; outreach, advocacy, life skills training, and housing search, and counseling services; outpatient health services; trauma counseling and victim services.

[c] Transitional housing is designed to provide housing and appropriate supportive services to homeless persons to facilitate movement to independent living within 24 months, or a longer period as approved by HUD.

[d] Emergency shelter is any facility with overnight sleeping accommodations, to provide temporary shelter for the homeless.

[e] Permanent supportive housing is long-term, affordable, community-based housing that is linked to appropriate supportive health and social services (e.g., substance abuse, mental health, case management, medical care services, and services for the disabled and frail elderly) that enable homeless individuals and homeless families with disabilities to maintain housing. There is no time limit to residency, provided a tenant meets the conditions of occupancy as established by the program.

Few Properties Deemed Suitable and Available for Homeless Assistance Were of Interest or Received Applications from Service Providers

Of the at least 10,000 properties determined to be suitable and available, approximately 1,200 properties received notices of interest, and we estimate that fewer than 400 properties received applications from homeless assistance providers, resulting in the transfer of 122 properties to assist the homeless in the 26 years since Title V's inception through March 2014 (see figure 3).

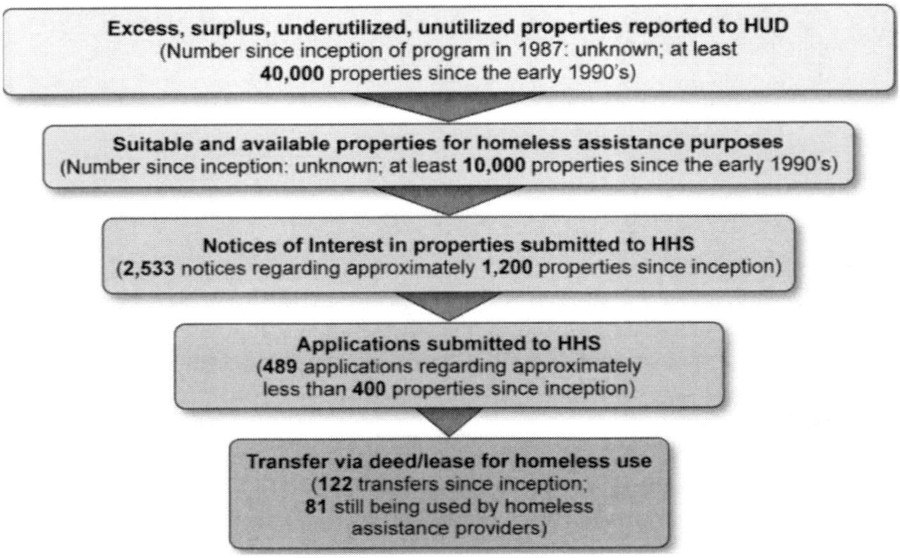

Source: GAO analysis of information from HUD officials and HHS data. | GAO-14-739.

Figure 3. Estimated Number of Properties Potentially Available for Homeless Assistance Compared to the Total Number of Properties Transferred under the Title V Homeless Assistance Program, 1987–2014.

Table 3. Examples of Suitable and Available Properties in 2013 That May Not be Practical for Homeless Assistance Use

Location	HUD description of property
Dublin, CA	Building, off-site use only: 30 square feet; control tower; poor conditions; restricted area; transferee must obtain real estate doc. to access/remove; contact Army for more information
West Sacramento, CA	Building: 3,840 square feet; 9 months vacant; poor conditions; restricted area; transferee will need anescort to access property
St. George Island, FL	Land: 0.34 acres; tower & fence needs to be removed; remote access; contact Air Force for more information
Ft. Benning, GA	Building, off-site removal only; 192 square feet; Sep Toil/Shower; poor conditions; secured area; contact Army for info. on accessibility/removal
Hawaii National Park, HI	Building, off-site removal only; 100 square feet; pollutant catch basin; poor conditions

Location	HUD description of property
Wahiawa, HI	Building, off-site use only: 512 square feet; storage; 46 yrs.-old; poor conditions
Johnston, IA	Building, remote/secured area: 3,076 square feet; family housing; 816+months vacant; deteriorated; escort required; contact Army for accessibility requirements
Mystic, IA	Building, off-site removal only; 80 square foot storage shed; one plus months vacant; deteriorated
Ft. Riley, KS	Building, off-site removal only; 128 square feet; latrine; deteriorating conditions; located on controlled area; contact Army for more information
Indian Head, MD	Building, off-site use only: 480 square feet; chemical plant 20+yrs. vacant; contaminated; major renovations required for other use
Smithville, MO	Building, off-site use only: 100 square feet; toilet needs extensive repairs
Lawton, OK	Building, off-site use only: 24,072 square feet concrete block/w brick
Stigler, OK	Building, off-site removal only; 24 square feet water well; poor conditions
Valliant, OK	Building, off-site removal only; 12 square feet; storage; flammable materials; poor conditions
Charleston, SC	Land: 5.59 acres; contamination; contact Navy for more information
Purdon, TX	Building, off-site use only: 624 square feet; 30+ years; restroom

Source: GAO analysis of HUD's 2013 Title V Annual Report. | GAO-14-739.

According to HHS data, since the inception of the program in 1987, most properties deemed by HUD to be suitable and which are available for homeless assistance have not received notices of interest or applications from homeless service providers. In addition, we found that in many cases, suitable and available properties may not have been practical for homeless service providers to use. Our analysis of HUD's 2013 annual report published in the Federal Register found 630 properties published as suitable and available including buildings ranging from a 12 square foot storage shed to a 75,720 square foot building in a restricted area, and vacant land ranging from about one hundredth of an acre to over 15 acres. These properties may be inconveniently located at a distance from existing communities or public transportation, within a military installation, or in poor condition—conditions consistent with what we found in our prior work (see table 3).[25]

As noted above, HUD is required to evaluate the properties and applies criteria that are defined in implementing regulations. A landholding agency may indicate on the Title V checklist, for example, that a property has extensive deterioration, but according to HUD officials, if the landholding agency does not provide supporting documentation, HUD may deem the property suitable for homeless assistance. As a result, HUD designates many properties as suitable with deficiencies that may therefore make them less desirable to homeless assistance providers. The suitability criteria in HUD's regulation for implementing the Title V homeless assistance program include provisions for excluding properties with deficiencies such as contamination, structural damage or extensive deterioration that are documented, extensive, and considered by HUD as representing a clear threat to personal safety. For example, while HUD did not determine conditions to rise to the level of a "documented deficiency," our analysis of the 630 suitable and available properties reported in the HUD's 2013 annual report found properties with conditions described as "deteriorated" (35 properties) and in "very poor condition" (18 properties).

Moreover, almost 80 percent of the properties published as suitable and available in 2013 were for "off-site use only." These properties refer to buildings and other removable structures that are located on land that is not surplus and, therefore, must be removed and relocated. According to officials from the National Law Center, the costs of moving the building, preparing the land on which to relocate the building, and making improvements needed to convert the building to provide services are often beyond the budget of the homeless-assistance service providers.

Officials from four of our nine selected landholding agencies told us they believe that properties for off-site use only are not practical for homeless assistance services. In addition, although an HHS official with responsibility for the Title V program told us that four of the 122 properties transferred under the Title V homeless assistance program were made available for off-site use only, these properties were trailers, which are designed to be easily moved, as opposed to other types of off-site properties described below, which may not be easy to move. For 2013, the most recent year reported, of the 630 properties HUD listed as suitable and available in the annual report, 78 percent were for "off-site use only" (see table 4).

Table 4. Number of Properties HUD Reported Suitable and Available for "Off-site Use Only"

Year of reporting	Total number of properties reported to HUD	Number of properties that were "Suitable/ Available"	Percentage of total that were "Suitable/ Available"	"Suitable/Available" properties that were for "off-site use only"	Percentage of "Suitable/Available" properties that were for "off-site use only"
2013 only	766	630	82%	489	78%
2008 –2013[a]	1,677	1,102	66%	859	78%

Source: GAO Analysis of HUD 2008-2013 Annual Reports published in the *Federal Register*. | GAO-14-739.

[a] Our analysis of HUD's annual reports published in the *Federal Register* for calendar years 2008 through 2013 identified 1,677 properties reported over the 6 years, of which 982 (59 percent) appeared in more than one annual report and 288 (17 percent) appeared in each of the six annual reports.

Since the majority of properties reported as suitable and available in 2013 were for off-site use only, as a result, they may be impractical for homeless assistance. For example, according to U.S. Army officials, since most of the Army's properties reported under Title V are located on secured installations and do not involve the transfer of land, these properties are often made available to homeless assistance providers for "off-site use only." In addition, because most buildings in the Army's inventory consist of masonry and steel, the removal of these properties is costly. As a result, U.S. Army officials said that very few homeless assistance providers have expressed interest in Army properties designated for "off-site use" since the program's inception.[26] Similarly, DOI officials told us that because the agency does not relinquish federal park lands, the buildings published as suitable and available located within federal parks are also designated for "off-site use only." Many federal park lands are in remote areas, and moving a building from those locations can be costly.

USICH's 2011 agency annual report stated that, because of the wide latitude in the suitability standard, a clear majority of the properties HUD finds "suitable" are not actually practical for homeless assistance.[27] As noted above, HUD considers all property suitable for homeless assistance unless a property's characteristics meet one or more of six conditions, such as national security concerns or location in a floodway. The relatively large numbers of properties deemed by HUD to be suitable and that were available may give homeless assistance providers, the public, and other stakeholders a false impression as to what properties are of practical use for homeless assistance because they included a large proportion of properties that have substantial deficiencies. In turn, this may mislead stakeholders about the extent to which the federal government is providing federal real property for homeless assistance.

An additional concern with HUD's Title V data lies in the limitations of its Title V database that HUD uses to store information on properties reported by landholding agencies and report them to the public. According to HUD officials, the agency has screened at least 40,000 properties since the early 1990s, of which at least 10,000 (at least 24 percent) were determined to be suitable and were available for homeless use (see figure 3). These estimates are based on HUD's Title V database, which was developed in the early 1990s, and maintains data on the properties reported to HUD by landholding agencies and HUD's suitability determinations.[28] However, HUD's database does not have the capability to generate reports on properties or data for the purpose of analyzing the properties reported for the Title V homeless assistance program. For example, when we asked HUD for reports from the database in order to perform our own analysis, such as the total number of properties reviewed for suitability and the total number published as suitable and available since program inception, the agency was unable to provide these data to us. The database was designed, and is primarily used, to generate listings of properties for publication in the *Federal Register*. The PDF format of the *Federal Register* reports poses challenges for automated analysis, and as a result, we had to manually count numbers of properties in specific categories to ensure the validity of our analysis, such as those for off-site use only reported in table 4. *Standards for Internal Control in the Federal Government* states that managers are responsible for providing reliable, useful, and timely information for transparency and accountability of programs and their operations.[29] Reliability also means that for any computer processing of the data elements used, the results are reasonable, complete, and accurate. In addition, federal information technology guidance for publicly available data states that accessible data should be made available in convenient, modifiable formats that can be retrieved, downloaded, indexed, and searched.[30] As the database cannot produce reports on the properties, HUD relies on hard-copy record keeping, which limits HUD's ability to make information on properties readily available, requiring labor intensive use of resources to find needed data. This capability is important because Title V requires HUD to make available to the public upon request all information in its possession about all properties reviewed and not identified as suitable for the homeless—about 30,000 properties according to HUD's estimate—including the reasons such properties were not so identified.[31] Moreover, HUD officials told us that during the recent litigation, the plaintiffs hired a contractor to make copies of the requested data from HUD's hard copy files, and it took three individuals several weeks to complete the task. Without a comprehensive database that maintains this information, HUD would need to respond to such a request on up to 30,000 properties by manually looking through files, which would not be an efficient use of resources. Because HUD uses the database primarily for generating listings, it has not assessed the extent to which the benefits of modifying the database to generate electronic reports for the purposes of responding to information requests or performing analysis, or if developing a new database to do so would outweigh the costs. Modifying its database, or developing a new one that is electronically searchable, would better position HUD to respond to information requests.

Landholding Agencies Report Many Properties That May Not Be Useful to Assist the Homeless, and Do Not Report Some Properties

While it is HUD's role to assess the suitability of properties for use to assist the homeless, some federal landholding agencies report many properties to HUD that may not, in the landholding agencies' estimation, be useful to assist the homeless. However, a few landholding agencies' officials told us that they do not report such properties or other surplus, underutilized, and unutilized properties because the reporting requirements are labor intensive or the properties may not be useful to the homeless. As noted above, the Title V homeless assistance program requires quarterly reporting and completion of a checklist for each property. The following examples illustrate the variety of Title V reporting practices among the agencies we reviewed.

- U.S. Navy officials told us that they report only excess properties to HUD because of the size of their real property portfolio—approximately 85 installations, and over 65,000 buildings and structures. According to these officials, the Navy does not have the resources to report on underutilized and unutilized property, which they said would require constant monitoring. Furthermore, the Navy also does not report some properties within Navy installations that do not allow public access within certain areas.

- US Army officials said that they report eligible Title V property to HUD but noted that the Title V process is time-intensive for several reasons. They noted that the Army may report up to 500 properties to HUD each quarter and that HUD requires submission of each property checklist in hard copy. In addition, U.S. Army officials said that the Army has to submit a Title V checklist each time it wants to demolish an installation building and that the Title V homeless-assistance program-reporting requirements could add about 6 months to the demolition process.
- DOE officials said that they report to HUD the property they are required to report, but believe that completing the Title V reporting requirement was not an efficient use of their resources since much of the agency's reported real property has documented deficiencies, including environmental contamination requiring remediation, and is located within secured boundaries and HUD determines many of these unsuitable for homeless assistance. For example, DOE properties typically include radiological contaminants commingled with other metals and chemicals associated with nuclear research and production. In our prior work, DOE also told us that the department understood the need to screen excess real property, but that much of its portfolio to be disposed had no remaining useful life and was most often located within a secure compound.[32]
- DOI officials said that they are required to—and do—report to HUD on numerous small, remotely located properties in National Parks that they have decided to dispose. For example, many cabins are not accessible by road or may be accessible only by water and only during certain times of the year. Officials also told us that in 2013, 73 properties, mainly small houses on National Park lands were determined suitable but for off-site use only, yet the majority of these properties were in such poor condition that they could not be moved. In addition, DOI officials said that they do not report to HUD real property that is only used seasonally as unutilized or underutilized because the agency will use the properties again in the following season. The Title V homeless assistance program checklist, however, expressly asks whether an underutilized property is used seasonally

(see app. II: HUD Title V Checklist Submitted to Landholding Agencies, item 6B).

- EPA officials noted that although some of its laboratories are only partially used, they do not report these as underutilized real property for HUD's Title V canvas because they do not believe they are required to do so. Rather, EPA's practice has been to report that it does not have any underutilized or unutilized properties for each quarterly canvass because the space is laboratory space that agency officials do not think is practical for homeless assistance programs. EPA officials said that they are currently conducting a space utilization study for laboratories, and after the study is completed, they will determine whether to report underutilized and unutilized properties identified through the study.
- GSA officials told us that as a provider of space to other federal agencies, GSA properties are sometimes temporarily or partially vacant as the space needs of tenant agencies fluctuate. GSA officials said that they do not consider these properties to be underutilized and unutilized because the agency plans to use them to house future federal tenants. GSA officials said that if they identified underutilized and unutilized property in the portfolio that was not to be reported as excess, they would report these to HUD's canvass. However, GSA could not identify any such properties that it had reported to HUD in the 6 years from 2008 through 2013. Nonetheless, even if GSA identified a future need for temporarily or partially vacant space, it, like other agencies, has two opportunities to inform HUD as to why reported properties may not be available: first, the HUD Title V checklist asks reporting landholding agencies to provide information on any current or anticipated limitations for using the property to assist the homeless for a period of one year or more; second, landholding agencies are required to provide statements to HUD on the availability of properties determined suitable, including reasons why the property cannot be declared excess or made available for use to assist the homeless.

HUD officials told us that they review and make a suitability determination only for those properties reported to them by landholding agencies and that they do not have a way of knowing how many properties should be, but are not reported. In 2013, the U.S. District Court for the District of Columbia noted that many landholding agencies appeared to be "failing to fairly and accurately" report Title V homeless assistance program-eligible properties as required under both the statute and Order.[33] Further, the court noted that there was a significant discrepancy between the numbers of properties reported to HUD under Title V and the much larger number of federal properties listed as "excess" or "underutilized" in other government reports and surveys. The District Court ordered several steps to ensure the proper reporting of properties including that GSA and HUD develop a plan for additional improved training programs for landholding agencies. To address the court order, GSA and HUD officials told us they conducted a joint webinar with HHS in November 2013 for landholding agencies.

HUD officials told us that they would prefer that agencies not be required to report certain types of properties at all because they may not be useful to assist the homeless. Requiring agencies to report all properties that fall within the four broad categories—excess, surplus, underutilized, and unutilized—may not be effective for certain types of properties. While there are discretionary elements in HUD's suitability criteria that are applied to properties submitted by the landholding agencies, HUD does not have the authority to release agencies from their statutorily required reporting of certain types of properties. Excluding certain types of properties such as "off-site use only properties" could enable HUD officials to focus on the suitable and available properties that may be more likely to assist the homeless and could help address issues of landholding agencies not reporting certain properties. In 2013, HUD proposed a revision to the law that would limit some of the types of properties agencies report, such as those that are located in high security areas and any building or structure that is made available for off-site use only. No action has been taken on that proposal.

HOMELESS ASSISTANCE PROVIDERS EXPANDED SERVICES, BUT SOME REPORTED ENCOUNTERING CHALLENGES IN IDENTIFYING, APPLYING FOR, AND USING REAL PROPERTY

Of the 11 homeless assistance providers we interviewed, the eight case study providers that acquired property cited benefits from the Title V program, such as expanding services and obtaining real property at no cost. These successes notwithstanding, the providers identified challenges such as locating information on available properties, a complex application, difficulty altering the approved use of transferred properties, and competing stakeholder interests. For example, although HUD reports properties in the *Federal Register* multiple times a year, and USICH provides links to them on its website, many homeless assistance providers may be unaware of the availability of properties. This may be because homeless assistance stakeholders have said the *Federal Register* is not user-friendly. Further, HUD's *Federal Register* reports list many of the same properties more than once. This may make listings even less user-friendly to providers. Homeless assistance providers and advocates we interviewed identified a number of actions that could address these challenges.

The Title V Homeless Assistance Program Enabled Selected Providers to Expand Services and Obtain Real Property at No Cost

Of the 11 homeless assistance providers we interviewed, the eight case study providers that acquired property cited a variety of benefits resulting from the acquisition of real property under the Title V homeless assistance program.[34] Representatives of the providers responsible for the eight case study properties we reviewed either said that the Title V program enabled them to expand their program or service capacity (five providers) or acquire real property at no cost (four providers). Representatives of two providers cited both types of benefits (see app. V for a description of each of the case study properties).

For example, the following providers spoke of how they were able to expand their programs through the Title V homeless assistance program:

- The acquisition of the former Boyle Heights Social Security Administration Building in Los Angeles enabled Volunteers of America of Los Angeles (VOALA) to offer services for the homeless, including referral services, food and clothing distribution, and job training in Los Angeles. VOALA reported serving more than 1,000 persons at this facility in 2013.
- The acquisition of an 84-acre portion of the former Homestead Air Force Base in Homestead, Florida, enabled Miami-Dade County to provide comprehensive services, including emergency shelter, transitional housing, and permanent supportive housing, in addition to job training, medical care, and clothing, among other services. In

2013, the Miami-Dade County Homeless Trust reported serving 2,143 homeless adults and minors at this facility.[35]

Other providers described how the Title V homeless assistance program enabled them to acquire property otherwise not affordable:

- Prior to acquiring four homes located in residential neighborhoods on Maryland's Eastern Shore, Crossroads Community, Inc. rented real property to provide rehabilitative services to individuals with mental illness in residential settings. Through the Title V homeless assistance program, the provider was able to replace rental property at a relatively low renovation cost with four homes that it acquired through the program. In addition, the program property allowed the provider to locate clients closer to its other service programs. According to Crossroads Community, Inc., the acquisition of the four houses currently saves the organization about $62,000 in rent on an annual basis.
- According to a representative of the City of Redmond, Washington, the greatest benefit of the Title V homeless assistance program lies in providing opportunities for non-profit organizations to acquire real property at minimal or no cost. The city acquired at no cost about half of a 10.2 acre site under the program that included 16 housing units formerly used to house U.S. Coast Guard personnel. The City of Redmond purchased the remainder of the real property through a negotiated sale with GSA. From the outset, the city planned to redevelop the Title V homeless assistance program portion of the real property into a larger facility to assist the homeless and 1-acre park, and develop the non-Title V portion into affordable housing units. Leveraging its resources, the city redeveloped the Title V homeless assistance program portion of the real property with 59 housing units that provided emergency, transitional, and permanent supportive housing for 319 households in 2013.

In addition to enabling homeless assistance providers to expand their services and obtain property they would likely have to pay for otherwise, the National Law Center stated that the Title V homeless assistance program also benefits the taxpayers by repurposing and reusing real property no longer needed by the federal government, helping the government—and by extension, the taxpayers—avoid and eliminate the maintenance and operation costs of retaining these properties.

Selected Homeless Assistance Providers Reported a Range of Challenges in Identifying, Acquiring, and Using Federal Real Property

These successes notwithstanding, homeless assistance providers we interviewed identified challenges such as locating information on available properties, a complicated application, difficulty altering the approved use of transferred properties, and competing stakeholder interests.

Most Selected Homeless Assistance Providers Were Unaware of Federal Register Notices

Although HUD reports regularly in the *Federal Register* for the purpose of informing homeless assistance providers about properties, among the 11 homeless assistance providers we interviewed, one said it was initially unaware of the program or the availability of real property in its area, and eight told us they eventually learned about the program through third parties rather than through the *Federal Register*. Title V requires HUD to publish, in the *Federal Register,* a list of real property it has evaluated for suitability. This occurs multiple times each year: four quarterly reports and a summary annual report. In addition, to comply with the 1988 court order, as modified in 1993, HUD publishes a weekly notice in the *Federal Register* of properties that are suitable and available, unavailable, and unsuitable (see table 5).

Table 5. Department of Housing and Urban Development's (HUD) *Federal Register* Reporting Requirements

Type of report	Time frame/ publication date	Purpose	Source authority
Reporting (general)	No later than 15 days after receiving reports from landholding agencies	Publish suitability determination of properties submitted to HUD by landholding agencies	42 U.S.C § 11411 (c)(1)(A).

Table 5. (Continued)

Type of report	Time frame/ publication date	Purpose	Source authority
Two *comprehensive* quarterly reports	End of 1st quarter – January 1 and End of the 3rd quarter – July 1	Publish newly reviewed properties as well as previously reported properties that may or may not have changes	42 U.S.C. § 11411 (c)(1)(A); *National Law Center on Homelessness and Poverty v. Veterans Admin., 819 F. Supp. 69* (D.D.C. 1993).
Two *supplemental* quarterly reports	End of the 2nd quarter and End of the 4th quarter – October 1	Publish only newly reviewed properties from the previous quarter	42 U.S.C. § 11411 (c)(1)(A); *National Law Center on Homelessness and Poverty v. Veterans Admin., 819 F. Supp. 69* (D.D.C. 1993).
Annual report	Previous calendar year/around February 15	Publish all the properties identified as suitable/available and suitable/ unavailable in the prior calendar year in addition to suitable properties from prior years that were republished and may still be available or for which the availability status has changed	42 U.S.C § 11411 (c)(1)(D), (c)(4)(B).

Source: GAO Analysis of 42 U.S.C §11411, National Law Center on Homelessness and Poverty v. Veterans Admin., 819 F. Supp. 69 (D.D.C. 1993) and HUD documents. | GAO-14-739.

HUD shares the *Federal Register* notices of suitable and available properties with the U.S. Interagency Council on Homelessness (USICH) multiple times a year, and USICH provides links to the list on its agency website. Nonetheless, according to national homeless advocates, many providers remain unaware of the availability of properties. For example, the National Law Center reported that despite the Title V homeless assistance program's having been in existence for 25 years, too few local government and homeless providers are aware that they are eligible to receive property free.[36] Moreover, a representative from the National Coalition for the Homeless told us that in general, homeless assistance providers do not have the staff resources to check the *Federal Register* consistently.

In addition, HUD's *Federal Register* reports list many of the same properties more than once, as required, and that may make listings more confusing and less useful for providers to use. For example, for the period from 2008 through 2013, 59 percent of the properties appeared in more than one annual report. Because, under Title V, suitable properties must be reported on an ongoing basis until they are disposed of—regardless of their availability status—HUD reports some properties in the *Federal Register* multiple times, in some cases over several years, even though homeless assistance providers have not expressed interest in these properties. Our analysis of HUD's annual reports for calendar years 2008 through 2013 found that of the 1,677 properties reported over the 6 years, 982 (59 percent) appeared in more than one annual report and 288 (17 percent) appeared in each of the six annual reports. For example, we found one property in Baltimore, Maryland, that was listed in three annual reports from 2011 through 2013. In another case in Macon, Alabama, a property was listed in HUD's annual reports each year from 2008 through 2011. In the past, some in Congress and the executive branch have expressed concern about reporting requirements; the basic concern has been that some requirements result in reports that may be unnecessarily burdensome to produce or, in some instances, not very useful. Our prior work at other federal agencies has reviewed reporting requirements, the limited usefulness of some reports, duplicative reporting, and has found that less frequent reporting could allow agencies to continue to fulfill their responsibilities.[37]

HUD officials told us that, instead of publishing suitable and available properties in the *Federal Register*, they believe it would be more efficient and beneficial to homeless providers to publish the information on their Community Planning and Development "OneCPD" website, which serves as a resource exchange and provides technical assistance to stakeholders for a wide variety of programs including the Title V homeless assistance program. Further, both the National Law Center and the National Coalition for the Homeless suggested that available properties should be listed on the Internet in an easily accessible format, unlike the *Federal Register*, which they said is not user-friendly. Some stakeholders suggested that the federal government could make information more accessible by establishing a single web-based source of information on the program. However, if HUD were to report Title V properties on its OneCPD website, this would add to HUD's other reporting requirements if the Title V reporting requirements remained unchanged, and HUD officials do not believe they have the resources to do both.[38]

Complex Application

Five of the homeless assistance providers we interviewed noted challenges with the application. Two providers reported that completing the application required additional resources and was time consuming, particularly in obtaining technical reports such as environmental assessments. For example, one organization hired a contractor to prepare the application, which was nearly 300 pages long and required extensive technical documentation. In another case, the representative said that the application process was time consuming because of the large volume of supporting documentation required. Among the homeless assistance providers we interviewed, one reported obtaining the environmental reports from GSA, while others paid a consultant to obtain the documentation or used their resources to collect it for the purpose of the application. Another provider noted that GSA responded slowly to requests for both access to the site and for documentation, such as site blueprints. According to this representative, GSA took nearly 60 days of the 90-day application period to provide access and documentation that had been requested at the beginning of the application process.[39] Based on our work, we believe the large difference, discussed above, between the number of notices of interest and the number of applications may be, in part, due to the complexity and resources required to complete the application within a 90-day period. These case study results are consistent with the National Law Center's findings, which state that the application is lengthy and cumbersome, making it difficult for a homeless assistance provider to complete in the short time frame imposed under the law. In addition, the application calls for homeless assistance providers to collect information that is already in the government's possession, such as a description of the easements on the property.[40] The HHS Title V official told us that several years ago, the Department modified the application packet to address some of these stakeholder concerns. Two homeless assistance providers we interviewed suggested that HHS consider providing examples of model applications on a public website. HHS officials told us that they believe posting examples of successful applications on the Internet may lead to homeless assistance applicants using examples that may not be relevant to their particular circumstances.

Difficulty Altering Approved Real Property's Use to Meet Changing Client Needs

HHS, as the agency responsible for ensuring that homeless providers use the transferred real properties according to the approved application, also approves any changes to the original program of use for the properties. Two of the selected case study providers told us that they found it difficult to alter the original program of use for their properties. According to the two providers, the needs of the homeless clientele they serve had changed since their applications were approved. For example, one provider told us that the homeless population the organization currently serves largely consists of persons recently released from incarceration and, unlike the population it served when the property was first transferred in 2002, is perhaps better educated than the previous population. This provider stated that due to the changing population, workforce training has become more of a need than it was in the past. The provider noted that it took many letters to convince HHS that workforce training was a necessary part of the organization's homeless assistance. Another provider obtained a property for use as transitional housing for mentally ill homeless adults and wanted to alter the program to provide permanent housing to this population; a representative for that provider told us that the organization has thus far decided not to pursue its request to HHS because it understands that it would have to restart the application process.[41] HHS Title V homeless assistance program representatives told us, that while much of the information requested for the original application would need to be resubmitted, the provider would not need to resubmit a full application.[42]

Competing Stakeholder Interests

Our literature review and case study interviews found that homeless assistance organizations often reported meeting resistance from local interests and groups when attempting to acquire federal properties. Further, USICH's 2011 annual report noted that, in some cases, local opposition to the use of the property by homeless providers has caused them to withdraw their applications to the Title V homeless assistance program.[43] Two of the homeless providers we interviewed for our case studies reported meeting strong community opposition, which, according to one provider, related to concerns about safety, number of homeless assistance facilities within a given area, and the impact on real property values, for example:

- One case study provider, whose real property is located in an industrial, non-residential area, told us that the organization changed its original plan from providing shelter services to providing job training and social services instead of shelter in response to local opposition from neighboring businesses.
- Another case study provider encountered strong local opposition to its proposal to use the four residential properties as locations for clients undergoing mental health rehabilitation. The provider said its organization mitigated the resistance over the course of a year by holding multiple informational community meetings and conducting a workshop on removing the stigma associated with mental illness and homelessness at a local community college. Since the program has been in place, the organization has not experienced any further opposition to the program.
- Another case study provider described how the organization successfully addressed and minimized the potential for local opposition. In this case, the City of Redmond, Washington, worked with an inter-local government organization– A Regional Coalition for Housing (ARCH)–in acquiring the Title V real property. The City and ARCH then worked with a consortium of homeless providers in developing a homeless assistance program. Anticipating concerns, particularly from nearby residents, ARCH and the city staff reached out to the neighborhood to ensure that neighborhood interests were represented during the planning phase of the program, including a series of meetings.

Our prior work has found similar competing stakeholder interests. For example, state and local governments, business interests in the communities where the assets are located, private sector construction and leasing firms, various advocacy groups, and the public in general have an interest in how the federal government carries out its real property management practices.[44] We have raised this concern as an underlying problem in our biennial high-risk area updates on federal real property.[45] In addition, we recommended to the Office of Management and Budget (OMB) in 2012, the development of a cohesive national strategy for managing federal excess and underutilized real property that would also address competing stakeholder interests. OMB did not directly state whether it agreed or disagreed with our recommendation.[46] Moreover, OMB has not taken action on our recommendation as of the time of this report.

All four federal agencies—GSA, HHS, HUD and USICH—bear some responsibility for addressing challenges homeless assistance providers face with the Title V homeless assistance program, such as identifying and acquiring properties and developing a web-based source of information on the program. By collaborating to address these concerns, the federal agencies could provide information that would be more useful to homeless providers and thereby more effectively manage agency resources to contribute to the goal to end homelessness. Our prior work has found that many of the meaningful results that the federal government seeks to achieve require the coordinated efforts of more than one federal agency and often more than one sector and level of government.[47] We have reported about the importance of collaboration among federal agencies for many years. In its 2011 annual report, USICH noted that the Title V homeless assistance program process for identifying properties, determining suitability, determining availability by landholding agencies, and leasing or deeding surplus properties involves at least three federal agencies and can appear quite confusing and cumbersome to homeless providers.[48] USICH is composed of representatives from 19 federal agencies—including GSA, HHS, and HUD. While not having the authority to ensure compliance, USICH monitors, evaluates, and recommends improvements in federal and state homeless assistance programs and is required by law to meet at least four times a year. USICH is supported by the Council Policy Group, which provides a regular forum for coordinating policies and programs, collecting data, developing special initiatives, and preparing recommendations for consideration by USICH members. Unlike other interagency groups, although USICH is a very small agency, it receives an appropriation from Congress and employs full-time staff in Washington, D.C., and five regional posts.[49] As such, resources and a process for addressing some of the stakeholder concerns are already in place.

CONCLUSION

HUD has evaluated at least 40,000 underused, unused, and unneeded federal real property assets for the Title V homeless assistance program since it began in 1987. However, only a small fraction of the properties HUD determined suitable and that were available have been transferred to homeless assistance providers since the program's inception—likely because the majority of the properties were not useful to them. The 81 active properties transferred have provided needed services to the homeless population across the nation. While HUD lists information on the properties it evaluates in the *Federal Register* multiple times each year, as required by law, many of the listings are duplicative, and many service providers are not even aware of the Title V homeless assistance program. Given that all underutilized, unutilized, excess, and surplus federal real property is subject to Title V homeless assistance program reporting requirements—including buildings, land, or both, without regard to location, size, or practicality—the scope of properties reported (with particular attention to the usefulness of the property and the frequency of reporting) is crucial to helping HUD make the program more useful to homeless assistance providers. In addition, a reliable, searchable electronic database of the properties HUD has reviewed would improve HUD's ability to provide information to meet required reporting needs. While homeless assistance providers benefitted from obtaining federal real property otherwise not affordable to them and expanded their services, addressing the challenges they face in identifying properties would improve program effectiveness. Collective efforts by all four responsible federal agencies—GSA, HHS, HUD, and USICH—could help to address these concerns. Without these changes, the Title V homeless assistance program may not be making the best use of its resources to make progress toward ending homelessness in the nation.

MATTER FOR CONGRESSIONAL CONSIDERATION

To ensure that properties determined as suitable and available are more likely to be practical for homeless assistance and that *Federal Register* reporting is not redundant, Congress should revisit the scope of properties to be reported to HUD with respect to the types of properties that may be less likely to be useful to assist the homeless and the frequency of *Federal Register* reporting.

RECOMMENDATIONS FOR EXECUTIVE ACTION

- To improve HUD's database on Title V homeless assistance properties, HUD should modify its existing database or create an electronic, searchable database to meet reporting needs to the extent that the benefits outweigh the costs.
- HUD, GSA, HHS, and USICH should work together to address the challenges that homeless assistance providers face with the Title V homeless assistance program by
- identifying what kinds of properties are most practical for homeless assistance, and
- developing a web-based source of information on the program for homeless assistance providers.

AGENCY COMMENTS AND OUR EVALUATION

We provided a draft of this report for review and comment to the four agencies with a role in administering the Title V homeless assistance program: GSA, HHS, HUD, and USICH. We also provided a draft of this report to the landholding agencies we included in our review: the EPA, the DOD service branches—the U.S. Air Force, the U.S. Army and the U.S. Navy—DOE and DOI. We received written comments from GSA, HHS, and USICH, which are summarized below. HUD's agency liaison provided comments via e-mail on September 18, 2014, which are summarized below. In addition, GSA, HHS, HUD, the U.S. Army and the DOE provided technical comments, which we incorporated as appropriate. The EPA, U.S. Air Force, U.S. Navy, and DOI did not provide any comments.

GSA concurred with the findings of the report and the recommendation that it work with HHS, HUD, and USICH to address the challenges that homeless assistance providers face by identifying what kinds of properties are most practical for homeless assistance and developing a web-based source of information on the program for providers. GSA stated that it will continue to work with both HUD and HHS on this effort. GSA noted that it has taken steps to enhance its website with additional information and resources about the Title V homeless assistance program and provide additional information about how to locate available properties. The agency stated that it has also provided the opportunity for interested homeless assistance providers to subscribe to receive automatic e-mail notifications as properties are posted to its website. These are positive steps to provide additional information on the homeless assistance program.

HHS did not concur with our recommendation that it should work together with GSA, HUD, and USICH to address the challenges that homeless providers face by identifying what kinds of properties are most practical for homeless assistance. HHS stated that this was outside of the scope of its legal authority and noted that under the authorizing statute and the regulation, HUD, is solely authorized to identify suitable property and apply the suitability criteria to properties reported by landholding agencies pursuant to Title V requirements. We recognize that under the statute,[50] HUD is solely authorized to make determinations regarding whether properties are suitable for use to assist the homeless. However, the McKinney-Vento Homeless Assistance Act, as amended, required GSA, HHS, and HUD to promulgate implementing regulations. In response, GSA, HHS, and HUD promulgated a joint interim final rule that set out, among other things, the criteria to be applied by HUD in making its suitability determinations. The interim final rule putting the joint regulation in place explained that the suitability criteria have been developed with the intent of excluding only those properties that are clearly unsuitable for use to assist the homeless. The issuing agencies of the joint rule may revisit the scope of such regulatory exclusions of clearly unsuitable property to assess if they merit adjustment. Given that the rule was a joint issuance by GSA, HHS, and HUD, our recommendation that the agencies work together to identify what kinds of properties are most practical for homeless assistance is directed to the four agencies with responsibility for implementing the program. HHS concurred with the second part of the recommendation that it should work together with GSA, HUD, and USICH to develop a web-based source of information on the program for homeless assistance providers, and noted that it is in the process of refurbishing its federal real property assistance website and will consult with the other three agencies to discuss options relating to web-based sources of information on the Title V homeless assistance program.

HUD also concurred with the report's overall findings, and with the recommendation that it modify its database or create a searchable, electronic database on the Title V homeless assistance properties to meet its reporting needs. HUD officials noted that its proposed legislative changes included the development of an improved database that would be searchable and would allow HUD stakeholders to view profiles of those properties that are suitable and available to be used to assist the homeless. HUD also concurred with the recommendation that it work together with GSA, HHS and USICH to address challenges providers face with identifying the kinds of properties that are most practical for homeless assistance, and to develop a web-based source of information on the program. HUD noted that it had already proposed legislative changes to create a web-based source of information on available properties in place of publishing properties in the *Federal Register*. Although we support a legislative change to address certain aspects of the law, as stated in our Matter for Congressional Consideration, our recommendations to HUD are not contingent upon legislative changes. As noted in our report, because HUD uses its Title V database primarily for generating listings for the *Federal Register*, it has not assessed the extent to which the benefits of modifying it to generate electronic reports, or developing a database to do so, would outweigh the costs. In addition, as one of the four federal agencies responsible for the program, HUD shares responsibility for addressing the challenges that homeless assistance providers face, such as identifying and acquiring properties and developing a web-based source of information on the program.

USICH agreed that the scope of properties that agencies are required to report under Title V include large numbers of properties that could not viably be used for homeless assistance. However, it did not agree with our recommendation that it work together with GSA, HHS, and HUD to identify the kinds of properties that are most practical for homeless assistance. USICH stated that improving the identification of properties that are practical for homeless assistance cannot occur through collaboration alone and that a legislative fix is an essential prerequisite. We continue to believe that, as one of the agencies responsible for implementing the Title V homeless assistance program, USICH shares responsibility for addressing challenges homeless assistance providers face, such as identifying and acquiring properties. As noted in our report, by collaborating to address these concerns, the federal agencies could provide information that would be more useful to homeless providers. USICH concurred with the recommendation on developing a web-based source of information on the program for homeless assistance providers and stated that it may be beneficial for disseminating information on available federal real properties to interested stakeholders.

David J. Wise
Director
Physical Infrastructure Issues

APPENDIX I: SCOPE AND METHODOLOGY

To determine what is known about the identification and transfer of federal real properties for homeless assistance under Title V, we reviewed the requirements of Title V of the Act as they apply to the General Services Administration (GSA), the Department of Health and Human Services (HHS), the Department of Housing and Urban Development (HUD), and the United States Interagency Council on Homelessness (USICH). We reviewed these agencies' internal policies, procedures and other documents on how they implement the requirements of the programs. HUD does not maintain electronic records of all the properties reported under Title V since the inception of the program. Thus, due to the lack of available data in a format that allowed analysis, HUD provided us with estimates of the number of underutilized, unutilized, excess, and surplus properties reported by landholding agencies and the number that HUD determined to be suitable and were available for homeless use from the early 1990s through March 31, 2014. These estimates are based on the number of properties that were entered into HUD's Title V database, developed in the early 1990s, several years after the McKinney-Vento Act was implemented. Further, HUD officials are not certain of the extent to which the database includes the Title V homeless assistance program properties reported prior to its creation. Due to the lack of available data in a format conducive to analysis, we could not verify the reliability of these estimates. We interviewed officials from HUD about how the estimates were derived and could not verify the reliability of these estimates. To assess the reliability of these estimates, we interviewed officials from HUD about how the estimates were derived and determined that the information provided by the agency provides a reasonable basis, with caveats, for reporting the number of properties that have been screened and published as suitable and available. In addition, to determine the number of properties reported in these categories and the number and percentage of these that were available for "off-site use only," we analyzed HUD annual reports of suitable/available and suitable/unavailable properties for years 2008 through 2013. This time frame was selected to include the 5 years prior to the audit, and when HUD's annual report for 2013 became available we added it to the analysis to include the most recent information. Our analysis of the *Federal Register* notices relied on identifying properties by the unique Property Identification (ID) number published with each property listing. We also obtained from HHS documents and data on the number of notices of interest and applications received for federal real property made available for homeless assistance and on the number, location, and use of properties transferred from the program's inception in 1987 through March 31, 2014—the date of the most recently available information.

To assess the reliability of these data, we interviewed officials from HHS about how the data are collected and maintained and the steps taken by the agency to ensure the completeness of these data. Based on this discussion, we determined that the data were sufficiently reliable for the purposes of this report. In order to assess the number of properties that received notices of interest and applications from interested providers, we also manually reviewed data on notices of interest and applications received to identify potential duplicate properties by GSA number, property name, location, and description. To understand how federal landholding agencies identify and report real property to HUD pursuant to the Act's requirements, we selected nine landholding agencies to include a range of size among real property portfolios of land and buildings. These agencies were GSA; HHS; the Departments of Defense's U.S. Army, U.S. Air Force, and U.S. Navy; the Departments of Energy; the Interior and Veterans Affairs;[51] and the Environmental Protection Agency. When combined, these nine landholding agencies accounted for almost 90 percent of the buildings held by the federal government in 2012.[52] We collected documents from these agencies to understand how each agency manages and fulfills its reporting requirements under Title V, the extent to which it collaborates with other agencies, and to obtain views on how Title V requirements impact the federal real property disposal process. We interviewed agency officials from the GSA, HHS, and HUD to understand how they process properties reported under Title V homeless assistance program requirements, and we interviewed officials from USICH to understand its role with Title V. We also interviewed agency officials from the nine landholding agencies to obtain their views on how they meet the Act's requirements and the impact of those requirements on each agencies disposal process.[53]

To determine the benefits and challenges selected homeless assistance providers and national advocacy organizations reported in identifying, acquiring and using federal real property, and the potential actions that could help address those challenges, we selected eight homeless assistance organizations that acquired federal real property under the program. The providers were: the City of Redmond, Washington; Crossroads Community, Inc.; Samaritan House; The Miami-Dade County Homeless Trust; Third Way Center; Urban Renewal Corporation; Veterans Coming Home/New Life Evangelistic Center; and Volunteers of America, Los Angeles. We made our selection using criteria such as the size of the real property acquired under the program, the services provided, geographic distribution, range of experiences with the Title V program, and suggestions from agencies and homeless advocacy organizations (GSA, HUD, HHS, USICH, the National Law Center on Homelessness and Poverty, and the National Coalition for the Homeless). In addition, to assist the selection, we also used information from news reports and our literature review to identify high-profile properties. We interviewed representatives from each of the selected organizations, reviewed their annual utilization reports, and conducted site visits to two properties transferred under Title V. While information from case studies is not generalizable, the perspectives of the homeless service providers provided us with examples of the benefits and challenges associated with the program. Further, to gain additional perspectives on experiences with the federal agencies and the application process, and identify potential improvements to the process, we convened a virtual discussion panel comprised of representatives from homeless assistance organizations whose Title V applications were not approved. We selected and recruited seven organizations, of which three agreed to participate in the panel.[54] These organizations were selected from HHS's Title V homeless assistance program applicant data from 2006 through 2013 based on their geographic locations and proposed use of the properties. We selected the particular time frame to ensure that the information provided was reasonably up to date. Since the virtual discussion panel was selected using a non-probability sample of homeless assistance applicants whose Title V applications were declined by HHS, like the case studies, their experiences cannot be generalized to all homeless service providers. In addition, we reviewed the reports and interviewed representatives of two national advocacy organizations—the National Law Center on Homelessness and Poverty and the National Coalition for the Homeless.

We conducted this performance audit from September 2013 to September 2014 in accordance with generally accepted government auditing standards. Those standards require that we plan and perform the audit to obtain sufficient, appropriate evidence to provide a reasonable basis for our findings and conclusions based on our audit objectives. We believe that the evidence obtained provides a reasonable basis for our findings and conclusions based on our audit objectives.

APPENDIX II: SAMPLE TITLE V CHECKLIST SUBMITTED BY LANDHOLDING AGENCIES TO HUD

TITLE V PROPERTY SURVEY
FEDERAL PROPERTY INFORMATION CHECKLIST
(REV. 11/89)

INSTRUCTIONS: 1) Use this form.
2) Complete all items below or the checklist will be returned for completion.

Date: ______________ Property ID # [______________]
(HUD will assign)

1. FEDERAL LANDHOLDING AGENCY: **Bureau:** ______________

2. PROPERTY (name): ______________

(installation name, if applicable): ______________

3. ADDRESS (street and number, or if none, a brief description of how to locate property)

4. GSA INVENTORY CONTROL NO. (if available):

5. PREVIOUSLY REPORTED TO HUD? ☐ Yes ☐ No

Determination by HUD (date:__________): ☐ Suitable ☐ Unsuitable

6. PROPERTY DESCRIPTION:

☐ Building ☐ Vacant Land ☐ Other (improved land)

A. Current status: ☐ Unutilized ☐ Underutilized ☐ Excess ☐ Surplus

If excess or surplus, GSA Disposal Control No.:

B. If underutilized, type of underutilization (describe):
☐ Portion ☐ Seasonal ☐ Intermittent ☐ Other (describe):

C. Predominant surrounding land use:

D. Unusual physical features or impediments:

E. Legal constraints (right of entry, covenants, permits, licenses, etc.):

F. Other (comments):

7. BUILDING DESCRIPTION:

A. Age:

B. Structure type:

C. Size (usable square feet per floor):

D. Number of floors:

E. Current or most recent use (storage, residential, office, etc.):

F. If currently occupied or leased, indicate:
i. Percentage of total space occupied or otherwise in use: ______ percent.
ii. Expiration date(s) of any existing lease(s) or renewal period(s):

F. If currently vacant, indicate number of months vacant: ________

8. BUILDING CONDITION: Meets or has the potential to meet the following criteria:

	MEETS		POTENTIAL	
	Yes	No	Yes	No
A. Operating sanitary facilities	☐	☐	☐	☐
B. Potable water	☐	☐	☐	☐
C. Electric power	☐	☐	☐	☐

D. Indicate (if known) distance to nearest utility hook-up(s):

E. Heating facilities adequate for climate	☐	☐	☐	☐
F. Structurally sound				
i. Foundation	☐	☐	☐	☐
ii. Floors	☐	☐	☐	☐
iii. Roofs	☐	☐	☐	☐
iv. Exterior walls	☐	☐	☐	☐
v. Interior walls	☐	☐	☐	☐

vi. Describe general condition or extent of repairs needed

9. VACANT LAND:

A. Size (acres, square footage):
B. Description of improvements (i.e. paved, etc.):

C. Current or most recent use:
D. If occupied, indicate:
 i. Percentage of total land area occupied or otherwise in use: ______ percent.
 ii. Expiration date of any existing lease or renewal period:

10. VACANT LAND CONDITION: Meets or has the potential to meet the following criteria:

	MEETS Yes	MEETS No	POTENTIAL Yes	POTENTIAL No
A. Operating sanitary facilities	☐	☐	☐	☐
B. Potable water	☐	☐	☐	☐
C. Electric power	☐	☐	☐	☐

D. Indicate (if known) distance to nearest utility hook-up(s):

11. ACCESS:

A. Does this property have public access? ☐ Yes ☐ No
 If yes, how (road, other):

 If no, indicate:
 i. Distance to the nearest road:
 ii. Type of terrain:
 iii. Miles to nearest town/city:

 Accessible by public transportation: ☐ Yes ☐ No
 Type of transportation:

B. Indicate any restrictions on access (hours, etc.)

12. ENVIRONMENTAL SUITABILITY:

A. Is the property subject to contamination by toxic or hazardous materials or waste?
 ☐ Yes ☐ No

 Identify the basis for determination (submit documents):

 If yes, also identify:
 i. Nature of contaminants:
 ii. Location of contaminants:
 iii. Extent (percentage of building or number of acres affected) of contaminants:
 iv. Any scheduled cleanup plans (include projected date of completion and estimate of cost, if known:

B. Is an industrial/commercial Federal facility handling flammable or explosive material (excluding underground storage) located on the property or within 2,000 feet of its boundary (exclude underground storage, gasoline stations, tank trucks, and any above-ground container(s) with a capacity of 100 gallons or less of such materials)?
☐ Yes ☐ No

If yes, indicate:
 i. Number of acres (herein being determined for possible use by the homeless) located **more than** 2,000 feet from such facility:

 ii. Nature of the facility and material:

C: Is any portion of the property located within an airport runway clear zone?
☐ Yes ☐ No

If yes, indicate the portion (percentage) of the property which is so located: ______ percent.

D. Is any portion of the property located within a 100 year floodplain? (note that the fact that a Federal property is not included in an existing floodplain map or study does not, by itself, justify a "No" answer.)
☐ Yes ☐ No

E. Is the property impacted by any other environmental condition which might jeopardize the safety of occupants of the property (e.g., friable asbestos, PCBs, radon, periodic flooding)?
☐ Yes ☐ No

Indicate:
 i. Basis for determination (submit document):

 ii. Nature of condition:

 iii. Extent of condition:

 iv. Location of condition:

F. Are there any other known environmental conditions which could affect or be impacted by the occupancy of the property (e.g., endangered species, wild and scenic rivers, wetlands, historic properties, storm water runoff; etc.)?
☐ Yes ☐ No ☐ Undetermined

If yes, for each:
 i. Describe the environmental condition:

 ii. Describe the potential impact:

 iii. Basis for the determination (submit document):

13. SECURITY:

A. Is the property located in a secure facility to which the general public is denied access?
☐ Yes ☐ No

B. If the answer above is yes, can alternative access be provided for the general public without compromising security requirements?
☐ Yes ☐ No

Indicate method of providing access:

14. LIMITATIONS ON USE:

A. Are there now, or are there anticipated to be, any other limitations not previously described on the use of this property to assist the homeless for a period of one year or more?
☐ Yes ☐ No

If yes, describe the limitation:

B. Does the limitation currently exist?
☐ Yes ☐ No

If no, when will any limitation take effect? ____________
(date of effect)

15. CHECKLIST CONTACT PERSON (name):

(title):

(phone number):

(email):

(date prepared):

☐ Yes ☐ No PHOTOS (not required) are attached?

☐ Yes ☐ No Additional amplifying information documents (not required) are attached?

APPENDIX III: LIST OF LANDHOLDING AGENCIES HUD CANVASSES FOR TITLE V

1. Central Intelligence Agency
2. Department of Commerce
3. Department of Agriculture

4. Department of the Air Force
5. Department of the Army
6. Department of the Navy
7. Department of Education
8. Department of Energy
9. Department of the Interior
10. Department of Justice
11. Department of Health and Human Services
12. Department of Labor
13. Department of State
14. Department of Transportation
15. Department of the Treasury
16. Department of Veterans Affairs
17. Environmental Protection Agency
18. Federal Communications Commission
19. Federal Emergency Management Agency
20. General Services Administration
21. International Broadcasting Bureau of the Broadcasting Board of Governors
22. National Aeronautics and Space Administration
23. National Science Foundation
24. U.S. Army Corps of Engineers
25. U.S. Coast Guard

APPENDIX IV: SERVICES PROVIDED AT 81 ACTIVE PROPERTIES TRANSFERRED UNDER TITLE V, BY STATE

As of March 2014, 81 Title V properties were currently in use by homeless assistance providers across the country to provide a range of homeless assistance services. The table below presents the services provided at each location by state.

Table 6. Services Provided at 81 Active Properties Transferred under Title V, by State

Homeless Provider, Location (by State)	Services														
	Supportive Services[a]	Transitional Housing	Referral Services	Emergency Shelter	Permanent Supportive Housing	Administrative Offices	Goods and Clothing Distribution	Education /Job Training	Daycare /Day Center	Food Distribution	Mental Health	Warehouse and Storage	Non-Use (Potential	Case Management	Total Number of Services
Catholic Social Services, Inc., Anchorage, AK		●			●										2
Tundra Women's Coalition, Bethel, AK		●													1
Tundra Women's Coalition, Bethel, AK		●													1
Salvation Army, Benton, AR	●			●											2
The Family Center, Inc., Helena, AR.						●									1
Quapaw House, Inc., Hot Springs, AR	●	●			●										3
Our House, Inc., Little Rock, AR	●	●		●					●						4
Esperanza en Escalante, Tucson, AZ	●	●	●												3
House of Refuge, Inc., Mesa, AZ	●	●													2
House of Refuge East, Mesa, AZ	●	●													2
The Community Housing Partnership, Inc., Mesa, AZ	●	●				●			●						4

Table 6. (Continued)

Homeless Provider, Location (by State)	Services														
	Supportive Services[a]	Transitional Housing	Referral Services	Emergency Shelter	Permanent Supportive Housing	Administrative Offices	Goods and Clothing Distribution	Education /Job Training	Daycare /Day Center	Food Distribution	Mental Health	Warehouse and Storage	Non-Use (Potential	Case Management	Total Number of Services
Community Social Model Advocates, Inc., Atwater, CA	●		●			●									3
Community Social Model Advocates, Inc., Atwater, CA							●								1
Salvation Army, Bell, CA	●	●	●	●		●					●				6
Shelter Partnership, Inc, Bell, CA							●								1
Salvation Army Southern California Division, Los Angeles, CA	●	●													2
Volunteers of America of L.A., Los Angeles, CA	●		●												2
Veterans Transition Center of Monterey, Marina, CA		●													1
Housing Authority of the County of Monterey, Monterey, CA												●			1

Homeless Provider, Location (by State)	Services														
	Supportive Services[a]	Transitional Housing	Referral Services	Emergency Shelter	Permanent Supportive Housing	Administrative Offices	Goods and Clothing Distribution	Education /Job Training	Daycare /Day Center	Food Distribution	Mental Health	Warehouse and Storage	Non-Use (Potential	Case Management	Total Number of Services
Housing Authority of the County of Monterey, Monterey, CA	●	●	●												3
Interim, Inc., Monterey, CA	●	●	●												3
Shelter Outreach Plus, Monterey, CA	●	●	●												3
Shelter Plus, Monterey, CA	●	●	●												3
Vietnam Veterans of Monterey County, Monterey, CA	●	●	●												3
County of Sacramento, Rancho Cordova, CA	●	●													2
Vietnam Veterans of California, Inc., Redding, CA													●		1
California Emergency Food Link, Sacramento, CA							●								1
Grace Apostolic Church, San Bernardino, CA							●								1
Grace Apostolic Church, San Bernardino, CA							●					●			2

Table 6. (Continued)

Homeless Provider, Location (by State)	Services														
	Supportive Services[a]	Transitional Housing	Referral Services	Emergency Shelter	Permanent Supportive Housing	Administrative Offices	Goods and Clothing Distribution	Education /Job Training	Daycare /Day Center	Food Distribution	Mental Health	Warehouse and Storage	Non-Use (Potential	Case Management	Total Number of Services
Third Way Center, Denver, CO		•													1
Community for Creative Nonviolence, Inc., Washington, D.C.								•							1
Metropolitan Dade County Government, Homestead, FL		•		•	•	•			•						5
Mount Olive Community Outreach Center, Inc., Albany, GA		•		•											2
Growing Home, Inc., Miller Township, IL								•							1
5020 State Street, LLC, St. Louis, IL	•	•	•												3
North Central-Flint Hill Agency on Aging, Manhattan, KS	•		•											•	3
Aftercare Ministries, Inc., Alexandria, LA													•		1
Monroe Area Guidance Center, Monroe, LA		•		•											2

	Services														
Homeless Provider, Location (by State)	**Supportive Services[a]**	**Transitional Housing**	**Referral Services**	**Emergency Shelter**	**Permanent Supportive Housing**	**Administrative Offices**	**Goods and Clothing Distribution**	**Education /Job Training**	**Daycare /Day Center**	**Food Distribution**	**Mental Health**	**Warehouse and Storage**	**Non-Use (Potential**	**Case Management**	**Total Number of Services**
City of Lynn, Lynn, MA						●				●					**2**
Crossroads Community, Inc., Chestertown, MA		●													**1**
Health and Education Services, Inc., Topsfield, MA	●				●										**2**
Vietnam Veterans Workshop, Inc., Boston, MA	●	●	●	●	●										**5**
Advocates for Homeless Families, Frederick, MD		●						●							**2**
Catholic Charities of the Archdiocese of Washington, Inc., Waldorf, MD	●		●		●										**3**
City of Bangor, Bangor, ME		●													**1**
AMHC Facilities, Inc., Caribou, ME	●		●		●										**3**
Homeworkers Organized for More Employment, Ellsworth, ME				●											**1**

Table 6. (Continued)

	Services														
Homeless Provider, Location (by State)	**Supportive Services[a]**	**Transitional Housing**	**Referral Services**	**Emergency Shelter**	**Permanent Supportive Housing**	**Administrative Offices**	**Goods and Clothing Distribution**	**Education /Job Training**	**Daycare /Day Center**	**Food Distribution**	**Mental Health**	**Warehouse and Storage**	**Non-Use (Potential**	**Case Management**	**Total Number of Services**
Pontiac Rescue Mission, Pontiac, MI	●	●	●	●											4
Salvation Army, Warren, MI	●			●		●									3
Salvation Army, Duluth, MN		●	●				●								3
Economic Security Corp. of Southwest Area, Joplin, MO	●		●												2
New Life Evangelistic Center, Inc., Springfield, MO			●					●							2
Human Resource Development Council, Inc., Bozeman, MT	●	●	●	●											4
Samaritan House, Inc., Kalispell, MT	●		●			●									3
Housing Authority of the County of Scottsbluff, NE, Scottsbluff, NE	●		●				●								3

Homeless Provider, Location (by State)	Services														
	Supportive Services[a]	Transitional Housing	Referral Services	Emergency Shelter	Permanent Supportive Housing	Administrative Offices	Goods and Clothing Distribution	Education /Job Training	Daycare /Day Center	Food Distribution	Mental Health	Warehouse and Storage	Non-Use (Potential	Case Management	Total Number of Services
Middlesex Interfaith Partners with the Homeless, Edison, NJ	●	●	●												3
Urban Renewal Corp., Kearny, NJ							●	●							2
New Day, Inc., Albuquerque, NM	●		●	●											3
Overcoming-Love Ministries, Brooklyn, NY	●	●													2
Paterson Coalition for Housing, Inc., Clifton, NY		●													1
Rockland Housing Action Coalition, Inc., Tappan, NY					●										1
Neighbors of Watertown, Inc., Watertown, NY	●		●		●										3
United Christian Ministries, Lawrenceville, PA	●	●	●												3
Community Mental Health Service Properties, Inc., Phoenixville, PA		●								●					2

Table 6. (Continued)

Homeless Provider, Location (by State)	Services														
	Supportive Services[a]	Transitional Housing	Referral Services	Emergency Shelter	Permanent Supportive Housing	Administrative Offices	Goods and Clothing Distribution	Education /Job Training	Daycare /Day Center	Food Distribution	Mental Health	Warehouse and Storage	Non-Use (Potential	Case Management	Total Number of Services
Community Mental Health Services. Inc., West Chester, PA			•			•									2
Interfaith Hospitality Network of York County, SC, Rockhill, SC	•	•	•												3
Wintergarden Women's Shelter, Carrizo Springs, TX	•		•	•											3
Union Gospel Mission, Dallas, TX	•	•													2
Woman, Inc., Galveston, TX	•	•	•												3
New Haven Home, Mineral Wells, TX	•	•	•	•											4
Concho Valley Center for Human Advancement, San Angelo, TX					•										1
City of San Antonio, San Antonio, TX	•		•	•	•										4
Central Piedmont Action Council, Inc., Farmville,VA			•			•									2

Homeless Provider, Location (by State)	Services														
	Supportive Services[a]	Transitional Housing	Referral Services	Emergency Shelter	Permanent Supportive Housing	Administrative Offices	Goods and Clothing Distribution	Education /Job Training	Daycare /Day Center	Food Distribution	Mental Health	Warehouse and Storage	Non-Use (Potential	Case Management	Total Number of Services
The Salvation Army, Lynchburg, VA									●						**1**
County of Prince William, Woodbridge, VA	●	●	●												**3**
NE Kingdom Community Action, Inc., Newport, VT			●			●									**2**
King County Housing Authority, Kent, WA	●	●	●	●	●										**5**
City of Redmond, Redmond, WA		●		●											**2**
Integrated Community Services of Parkersburg, Parkersburg, WV	●		●	●											**3**
Northwood Health Systems, Inc., Wheeling, WV			●	●							●				**3**
Wyoming Coalition for the Homeless, Cheyenne, WY								●	●						**2**
Total Number of Services	**43**	**42**	**37**	**19**	**12**	**11**	**8**	**6**	**5**	**2**	**2**	**2**	**2**	**1**	**192**

Source: GAO analysis of HHS information. | GAO-14-739

APPENDIX V: EIGHT HOMELESS ASSISTANCE CASE- STUDY PROPERTIES

California

Volunteers of America of Los Angeles (VOALA) is a non-profit human services organization committed to serving people in need, strengthening families, and building communities. The property consists of a single-story masonry building in very good condition. VOALA offers several homeless assistance programs at the site including Early Head Start, which provides comprehensive services to homeless families with children under 4 years of age; Incarcerated Veterans Transition Program, which provides employment support for veterans about to be released or just released from incarceration; Female & Single Head of Household, which provides case management services to female and single head-of- household veterans; and Supportive Services for Veteran Families, which provides a housing placement program. According to VOALA, the four programs served 1,029 individuals in 2013.

Property Name:	Boyle Heights Social Security Building
Location:	Los Angeles, California
Property Description:	1 building; .95 acre
Notice of interest date:	2/3/2009
Application date:	3/31/2009
Year transferred:	12/14/2009 (deed conveyance)
Grantee:	Volunteers of America, Los Angeles
Homeless Assistance Use:	Supportive and referral services

Source: GAO|GAO-14-79.

Figure 4. Former Social Security Administration Building.

Colorado

Third Way Center is a non-profit organization that provides transitional housing and round-the-clock psychiatric care for at-risk youth in Denver, CO. The property was originally part of the Lowry Air Force Base, which closed as a result of the Base Realignment and Closure Act (BRAC) in 1991. Since the property became available as a result of a pre-Redevelopment Act BRAC action, it was subject to Title V Homeless Assistance Program reporting requirements. According to HHS, one factor in the long period between the base closure and when the property became available was the environmental clean-up that was required at the site. When Third Way acquired the property in 2003, the property consisted of a one-story building that the provider subsequently demolished to construct four residential homes. The organization uses this property to provide a number of services to homeless adolescents—including shelter, meals, job training, mental health treatment, and an on- site, state-approved high school.

Property Name:	**Lowry Air Force Base Building**
Location:	Denver, Colorado
Property Description:	1 building (6,800 square feet); 1.8 acres
Notice of interest date:	10/06/1999
Application date:	1/06/2000
Year transferred:	6/03/2003 (deed conveyance)
Grantee:	Third Way Center
Program Use:	Includes shelter, job training, and education

Source: Third Way Center, Denver, Co. | GAO-14-739.

Figure 5. Former Lowry Air Force Base Building.

Florida

The Miami-Dade County Homeless Trust is an organization within the Miami-Dade County government that is responsible for coordinating local homeless systems of care. The organization applied for and was conveyed 84 acres of unimproved land from the former Homestead Air Force Base, which was closed as a result of the Base Realignment and Closure Act in 1993. Since then, Miami-Dade Homeless Trust has developed the property, including a 300-bed emergency housing facility, a 192-bed transitional housing facility, and a 580-bed facility for families with individuals having disabling conditions. Services at these facilities include case management, adult and vocational education, job training, and various medical services. There is also a working farm and farmer's market on the property. According to Miami-Dade Homeless Trust, homeless assistance was provided at the property to more than 2,000 individuals in 2013.

Property Name:	**Homestead Air Force Base**
Location:	Homestead, Florida
Property Description:	0 buildings; 84.2 acres
Notice of interest date:	12/22/1993
Application date:	11/16/1995
Year transferred:	6/28/1996 (deed conveyance)
Grantee:	The Miami-Dade County Homeless Trust
Program Use:	Includes shelter, education, and mental health treatment

Source: Miami-Dade Homeless Trust, Miami-Dade County, FL. | GAO-14-739.

Figure 6. Former Homestead Air Force Base.

Maryland

Crossroads Community, Inc. is a nonprofit organization that provides a full array of psychiatric rehabilitation and case management services to adults and children through five counties on Maryland's Eastern Shore. The property consists of two raised foyer and two ranch homes located in Chestertown, Maryland, but the houses are not contiguous to each other. All four houses are being utilized as residences for a Residential Rehabilitation Program licensed by the State of Maryland. The program provides for licensed, supervised transitional housing for homeless adults who have mental illness. The people served are expected to transition to a less supervised setting within 24 months. Crossroads Community, Inc. initially met strong local opposition to its application and program as a result of an unrelated crime that occurred several years prior to the property becoming available. The organization was able to overcome opposition through a combination of informational meetings and a workshop at a local community college. Crossroads Community, Inc would like to convert at least two of the houses to permanent supportive housing sometime in the future.

Property Name:	**Stillpond Housing Units, U.S. Coast Guard (4 homes)**
Location:	Chestertown, MD
Property Description:	4 homes (each approx 1,100 square feet); 1.32 acres
Notice of interest date:	1/31/2002
Application date:	5/10/2002
Year transferred:	8/13/ 2002 (deed conveyance)
Grantee:	Crossroads Community, Inc., Centreville, MD
Homeless Assistance Use:	Transitional housing for adults in mental health rehabilitation programs.

Source: GAO. |GAO-14-739.

Figure 7. Former U.S. Coast Guard Family-Housing Site.

Missouri

Veterans Coming Home Center is a program of New Life Evangelistic Center (NLEC), non-denominational, faith-based organization headquartered in St. Louis, MO. Although NLEC initially wanted to use this property as emergency shelter for homeless veterans, it was unable to win the approval of local authorities for this purpose. As an alternative, NLEC developed the property as a daytime respite center, providing access to food and hot beverages, laundry services, free clothing, and referral services, among other services. According to an NLEC representative, Veterans Coming Home expanded its outreach to all members of the homeless population in 2008, its second year of operation at the recommendation of HHS. In addition, beginning in 2012, Veterans Coming Home introduced counseling and case management services through partnerships with other organizations. According to the annual report submitted to HHS, Veterans Coming Home provided services to 421 homeless persons in 2013.

Property Name:	**Social Security Administration Building**
Location:	Springfield, Missouri
Property Description:	1 building (17,346 square feet); 1.08 acres
Notice of interest date:	11/1/2005
Application date:	1/30/2006
Year transferred:	9/5/2007 (deed conveyance)
Grantee:	Veterans Coming Home/New Life Evangelistic Center
Homeless Assistance Use:	Daytime respite center for homeless adults; case management

Source: New Life Evangelistic Center, Springfield, MO. | GAO-14-739.

Figure 8. Former Social Security Administration Building.

Montana

Samaritan House is a non-profit organization that has provided assistance to the homeless population in Kalispell, MT since 1991 through its several facilities. The organization uses this particular property, which consists of a main building and garage, to provide case management, job training, tutoring, meetings, and food, clothing and furniture distribution. According to Samaritan House, the acquisition of this property enabled an increase in capacity at its transitional housing facility by moving some of the operations that had been housed there to this facility, resulting in the addition of 13 beds. According to Samaritan House, the facility was used to provide homeless assistance to more than 1,100 individuals in 2013.

Property Name:	**Sonstelie Hall Army Reserve Center**
Location:	Kalispell, Montana
Property Description:	2 buildings (13,100 square feet and 750 square feet); 2.42 acres
Notice of interest date:	11/5/2007
Application date:	12/06/2007
Year transferred:	7/18/2008 (deed conveyance)
Grantee:	Samaritan House
Program Use:	Administrative offices, case management, job training.

Source: Samaritan House, Kalispell, MT. |GAO14-739.

Figure 9. Former Sonstelie Hall Army Reserve Center.

New Jersey

The Urban Renewal Corp. is a community-based, non-profit organization providing a variety services to vulnerable populations in New Jersey. This property consists of a four-story building that was formerly used as a Naval Reserve Center. The building is currently used to provide the homeless with job training and education, in addition to a variety of social services, such as substance abuse and HIV/AIDS counseling, and case management. Initially, the Urban Renewal Corp. had intended to use the property as a homeless shelter, but after facing strong local opposition, it revised its intended program of use to include only non-shelter services to the homeless. Although it is not formally used as a shelter, the provider is authorized to use the facility as a warming station during the winter months to house up to 20 homeless people per night when outside temperatures fall below a certain point.

Property Name:	**Naval Reserve Center**
Location:	Kearny, New Jersey
Property Description:	1 building (about 50,000 square feet); 2.63 acres
Notice of interest date:	4/26/2001
Application date:	6/27/2001
Year transferred:	3/27/2002 (deed conveyance)
Grantee:	Urban Renewal Corp.
Program Use:	Workforce development, GED training, and warming station during winter months

Source: Urban Renewal Corp., Keamy, NJ. |GAO-14-739.

Figure 10. Former Naval Reserve Center.

Washington

When the City of Redmond learned that federal real property would become available for homeless assistance within its boundaries, it retained an "inter-local" governmental organization that it is a member of, A Regional Coalition for Housing (ARCH), to assist the city in preparing an application and developing a program for the property. The property consisted of a 5.1 acre parcel including 18 residences that had been used to house U.S. Coast Guard staff. The city contracted with a consortium of four homeless assistance providers to rehabilitate and operate the existing units for transitional housing on 4.1 acres of the site, reserving the remaining acre for a recreational area. In 2003, the consortium demolished the original units and replaced them with new buildings that included a total of 59 housing units to provide transitional housing for the homeless. According to the City of Redmond's most recent Annual Utilization Report to HHS, the property, now called Avondale Park, provided emergency shelter and transitional housing in calendar year 2013 to 319 individuals.

Property Name:	**U.S. Coast Guard Family Housing Site**
Location:	Redmond, Washington
Size:	18 Buildings; 5.1 acres
Notice of interest date:	7/5/1996
Application date:	11/15/1996
Transfer Date:	9/25/1997 (deed conveyance)
Grantee:	City of Redmond, Washington
Homeless Assistance Use:	Emergency shelter; transitional housing; case management

Source: City of Redmond, Redmond, WA. |GAO-14-739.

Figure 11. Former U.S. Coast Guard Housing.

End Notes

[1] U.S. Department of Housing and Urban Development, *The 2013 Annual Homeless Assessment Report (AHAR) to Congress*, (Washington, D.C.: 2013). Of the 610,042, 394,698 people were homeless in sheltered locations and 215,344 were living in unsheltered locations.

[2] National Law Center on Homelessness and Poverty. *This Land Is Your Land: How Surplus Federal Property Can Prevent and End Homelessness* (Washington, D.C.: October 2013).

[3] GAO, *Federal Real Property: The Government Faces Challenges to Disposing of Unneeded Buildings*. GAO-11-370T (Washington, D.C.: Feb. 10, 2011).

[4] GAO, *High Risk Series: An Update*. GAO-13-283 (Washington, D.C.: February 2013).

[5] Pub. L. No. 100-77, 101 Stat. 482 (1987). The Stewart B. McKinney Homeless Assistance Act, enacted in 1987, was renamed the McKinney-Vento Homeless Assistance Act in October 2000 by Pub. L. No. 106-400, 114 Stat. 1675 (2000). For the purposes of this report, we will refer to this program as the Title V homeless assistance program.

[6] GAO, *Federal Real Property: Progress Made Toward Addressing Problems, but Underlying Obstacles Continue to Hamper Reform*, GAO-07-349 (Washington, D.C.: Apr. 13, 2007).

[7] After preliminary audit work, we did not continue our work at VA because we learned that very little of VA's property becomes available for Title V purposes.

[8] Altogether, GSA, HHS, and the other seven landholding agencies we reviewed account for almost 90 percent of real property held by the federal government in 2012. According to HUD officials, HUD is not a landholding agency.

[9] The national advocacy organizations were the National Coalition for the Homeless and the National Law Center on Homelessness and Poverty.

[10] A "landholding agency" is a federal department or agency with the statutory authority to control real property. 42 U.S.C. § 11411(i)(3).

[11] See app. III for a list of the 25 landholding agencies HUD currently canvasses.

[12] 24 C.F.R. § 581.6 (a); 41 C.F.R. § 102-75.1185(a); 45 C.F.R. § 12a.6(a).

[13] 42 U.S.C § 11411(b), (c).

[14] 24 C.F.R. § 581.5(c); 41 C.F.R. § 102-75.1180(c); 45 C.F.R. § 12a.5(c).

[15] If the application is for a deed conveyance of the property (meaning that the title of the property passes from the government to the grantee) as opposed to a lease, the private sector organizations must be incorporated under section 501(c)(3) as tax-exempt organizations.

[16] Written notice of intent to apply for a property may also be filed after the 60-day holding period. Such applications may be approved if the property remains available for homeless assistance use.

[17] 42 C.F.R. § 581.5(f); 41 C.F.R. § 102-75.1180(f); 45 C.F.R. § 12a.5(f).

[18] 45 C.F.R § 12a.9(e)(2).

[19] According to HHS, reversion for reasons of noncompliance is typically a measure of last resort and undertaken only when other attempts at bringing the grantee into compliance or a retransfer to another provider have failed.

[20] Pub. L. No. 103-421, 108 Stat. 4346.

[21] Pub. L. No. 101-510, 104 Stat. 1485,1808.

[22] Such properties are subject to a process that involves Local Redevelopment Authorities' (LRA) consultation with representatives of the homeless in the communities in the vicinity of the installation concerned to determine the need for homeless assistance and how portions of the former military installations might be used to meet it. LRA redevelopment plans are reviewed by HUD. Homeless assistance providers apply to the LRA for property on such installations that might be used to assist the homeless.

[23] The Federal Real Property Profile, created pursuant to Executive Order 13327, is the federal government's inventory system that is to contain data on all real property assets within and outside the United States, including improvements on federal land. Executive Order No. 13327, *Federal Real Property Asset Management*, 69 Fed. Reg. 5897 (Feb. 6, 2004).

[24] *Federal Property Disposal*: Hearing before the House Committee on Oversight and Government Reform, 112th Cong. (2011) (statement of Ms. Maria Foscarinis, Executive Director, National Law Center on Homelessness & Poverty).

[25] GAO, *Federal Real Property*: *Most Public Benefit Conveyances Used as Intended, but Opportunities Exist to Enhance Federal Oversight.* GAO-06-511 *(Washington, D.C.: June 21, 2006)*

[26] According to our analysis of HHS data, properties made available for "off-site use only" received fewer than 30 notices of interest from 1988 through March 31, 2014.

[27] United States Interagency Council on Homelessness. *Opening Doors: Appendix: Programs for People Experiencing Homelessness* 2011 (Washington, D.C.: 2011).

[28] HUD officials were uncertain when in the early 1990s the database was created and about the number of properties that were added to the database screened prior to its creation.

[29] GAO, *Standards for Internal Control in the Federal Government*, GAO/AIMD-00-21.3.1 (Washington D.C.: November 1999).

[30] Executive Order No. 13642, *Making Open and Machine Readable the New Default for Government Information*, 78 Fed. Reg. 28111 (May 14, 2013).

[31] 42 U.S.C.

[32] GAO, *Federal Real Property: Progress Made Toward Addressing Problems, but Underlying Obstacles Continue to Hamper Reform.* GAO-07-349 (Washington, D.C: Apr. 13, 2007). §11411(c)(1)(C)

[33] See Court Order accompanying *National Law Center on Homelessness and Poverty v. Veterans Admin*., 931 F. Supp. 2d 167, 174 (D.D.C. 2013).

[34] Altogether, we interviewed 11 homeless assistance providers, including representatives from eight case study properties that were acquired under Title V and three providers whose applications for property were not approved by HHS.

[35] The Miami-Dade County Homeless Trust is an organization within the Miami-Dade County government that is responsible for coordinating local homeless systems of care.

[36] National Law Center on Homelessness and Poverty. *This Land Is Your Land: How Surplus Federal Property Can Prevent and End Homelessness* (Washington, D.C.: October 2013).

[37] See for example, GAO, *Video Marketplace: Competition Is Evolving, and Government Reporting Should Be Reevaluated.* GAO-13-576 (Washington, D.C.: June 25, 2013), and GAO, *K-12* Education: Selected States and School Districts Cited Numerous Federal Requirements As Burdensome, While Recognizing Some Benefits. GAO-12-672 (Washington, D.C.: June 27, 2012).

[38] HUD has taken steps to help homeless assistance providers learn about properties such as a listserv and a call-in line that providers can use to obtain information about properties.

[39] According to the implementing regulations, HHS is to assist applicants in obtaining any pertinent environmental information in GSA, HUD or any other landholding agency's possession. 45 C.F.R. §12a.9(b)(8).

[40] National Law Center on Homelessness and Poverty. *This Land Is Your Land: How Surplus Federal Property Can Prevent and End Homelessness* (Washington, D.C.: October 2013).

[41] HHS concluded in 1992 that long-term housing did not constitute an appropriate use of property authorized under Title V and subsequently adopted the HUD standard, limiting occupancy to 24 months. However, HHS revised this policy effective September 1, 2006, to include permanent supportive housing, i.e., long-term, affordable housing that is linked to appropriate supportive health and social services that enable homeless individuals and homeless families with disabilities to maintain housing. 71 Fed. Reg.38882. (July 10, 2006).

[42] HHS officials noted that it requires the grantees wishing to change their approved program to address similar questions for the change as were required in the initial application. For example, the grantee must identify the need for the revised program and the funding available to implement the change. This information is used by HHS to make a determination on the need for the revised program within the community and if it is sustainable for the duration of the deed or lease.

[43] United States Interagency Council on Homelessness. *Opening Doors: Appendix: Programs for People Experiencing Homelessness 2011* (Washington, D.C.: 2011).

[44] GAO-07-349.

[45] GAO-13-283.

[46] GAO-12-645.

[47] GAO, *Managing for Results: Key Considerations for Implementing Interagency Collaborative Mechanisms,* GAO-12-1022 (Washington, D.C.: Sept. 27, 2012).

[48] United States Interagency Council on Homelessness. *Opening Doors: Appendix: Programs for People Experiencing Homelessness* 2011 (Washington, D.C.: 2011).

[49] GAO, *Managing for Results: Implementation Approaches Used to Enhance Collaboration in Interagency Groups,* GAO-14-220 (Washington, D.C.: Feb. 14, 2014).

[50] 42 U.S.C. §11411.

[51] After preliminary audit work, we did not continue our work at VA because we learned that very little of VA's property becomes available for Title V purposes.

[52] According HUD officials, HUD is not a landholding agency.

[53] We excluded from this report facilities on military bases closed after 1994 and subject to the provisions of the Base Closure Community Redevelopment and Homeless Assistance Act of 1994 (Redevelopment Act) (Pub. L. No.103-421, 108 Stat. 4346) but are reviewing implementation of the Act's provisions separately and will report on this in 2015.

[54] Representative of the other four organizations were unable to participate because of unanticipated schedule conflicts.

In: Unused Federal Property ...
Editor: Julia L. Brown

ISBN: 978-1-63482-995-3

Chapter 2

OVERVIEW OF FEDERAL REAL PROPERTY DISPOSAL REQUIREMENTS AND PROCEDURES*

Garrett Hatch, Daniel H. Else, Linda Luther, David M. Bearden and Kristina Alexander

SUMMARY

The federal government holds thousands of properties that agencies no longer need to accomplish their missions. When the government disposes of unneeded properties—through transfer, donation, or sale—it generates savings by eliminating maintenance costs. In addition, when state or local governments, nonprofits, or businesses acquire unneeded federal properties, they may be used to provide services to the public, such as temporary housing, or contribute to economic development.

The General Services Administration (GSA) plays a central role in disposing of unneeded property at most federal agencies. The Federal Real Property and Administrative Services Act of 1949 (Property Act) gives GSA the authority to dispose of real property at all federal agencies unless they have independent statutory authority to dispose of their own properties themselves. A number of agencies have independent disposal authority—ranging from limited to broad in scope—including two of the

* This is an edited, reformatted and augmented version of a Congressional Research Service publication R43818, prepared for Members and Committees of Congress dated December 10, 2014.

largest federal landholders, the U.S. Postal Service (USPS) and the Department of Defense.

When an agency notifies GSA that it has unneeded real property, GSA first offers to transfer the property to another federal agency, which must pay fair market value for it. If no other agency wishes to acquire the property, GSA may then convey it to a state or local government, or a qualified nonprofit, for up to a 100% discount—provided it is used for an approved public benefit. Should a state or local government or qualified nonprofit wish to acquire the property for a use other than one of the approved public benefits, GSA has the option to sell the property to them at fair market value. Finally, if the property is not sold to a public or nonprofit entity, it is offered for sale to the public.

The disposal of a federal property may be subject to a number of environmental requirements and historic preservation mandates, although which requirements apply depends on a number of site-specific conditions. Three principal federal statutes govern the environmental review process, identification and remediation of hazardous substances, and historic preservation: the National Environmental Protection Act (NEPA), the Comprehensive Environmental Response, Compensation and Liability Act of 1980 (CERCLA), and the National Historic Preservation Act (NHPA).

Among the agencies with independent statutory disposal authority, USPS has the greatest autonomy. The Postal Service has, in essence, been granted the authority to dispose of its properties as it deems appropriate, without the assistance of GSA. DOD also has independent statutory disposal authority, but of a more limited scope. DOD must use GSA to dispose of all properties that do not otherwise fall under the scope of special, temporary disposal authorities, commonly referred to as Base Realignment and Closure (BRAC) legislation.

INTRODUCTION

Federal executive branch agencies hold an extensive real property portfolio that includes more than 871,000 buildings and structures, and 40 million acres of land worldwide.[1] These assets have been acquired over a period of decades to help agencies fulfill their diverse missions. Agencies hold properties with a range of uses, including barracks, health clinics, warehouses, laboratories, national parks, boat docks, and offices. As agencies' missions change over time, so, too, do their real property needs, thereby rendering some assets less useful or unneeded altogether. Healthcare provided by the Department of Veterans Affairs (VA), for example, has shifted in recent decades from predominately hospital-based inpatient care to a greater reliance on clinics and outpatient care, with a resulting change in space needs.[2] Similarly, the Department of Defense (DOD) reduced its force structure by 36% after the Cold War ended, and has engaged in several rounds of base realignments and installation closures.[3]

Real property disposition is the process by which federal agencies identify and then transfer, donate, or sell facilities and land they no longer need. Disposition is an important asset-management function because the costs of maintaining unneeded properties can be substantial. In FY2013, for example, the government disposed of 21,464 unneeded properties with annual operating costs of $411 million.[4] Savings generated by the disposal of unneeded properties might be applied to pressing real property needs, such as improving building security or repairing existing facilities, or towards other pressing policy issues, such as reducing the national debt. Disposition is also important because it is a mechanism by which state and local governments, nonprofit organizations, and businesses may acquire federal property. In the hands of nonfederal entities, the previously underutilized properties may be used to provide services to the public, such as temporary housing, or contribute to economic development.

This report begins with an explanation of the central role played by the General Services Administration (GSA) in the disposal of federal real property at most agencies. It then provides a discussion of the unique disposal processes at DOD and the U.S. Postal Service (USPS), which each have independent statutory authority to dispose of their own properties. It concludes with an overview of the environmental and historic preservation requirements that apply to the disposal of properties at all federal agencies.

Centralized Disposal Through the General Services Administration[5]

The Federal Real Property and Administrative Services Act of 1949 (Property Act) applies to real property held by most federal agencies.[6] The Property Act gives GSA the authority to dispose of real property that federal agencies no longer need, although some agencies have been granted the authority to dispose of some or all of their own property.[7] Under the provisions of the Property Act, GSA disposes of federal real property for federal agencies that lack independent statutory authority to do so themselves. Agencies without independent disposal authority generally follow the process described in this section. The disposal processes at two landholding agencies with broad independent disposal authority, DOD and USPS, are also discussed in this report.

Federal Transfer

In order to identify properties that agencies no longer need, each agency is required to conduct an annual survey of its real property holdings. Properties that are no longer needed are reported to GSA as "excess."[8] GSA then physically inspects each excess property and hires a licensed appraiser to evaluate its fair market value.[9] Next, GSA sends a written Notice of Availability describing the property to other federal agencies and posts information about the property on its Property Disposal Resource Center website.[10] Agencies may also identify unneeded assets available for transfer through the Federal Real Property Profile (FRPP), a database of the buildings, structures, and land held by federal agencies.[11] If an agency wants to acquire an excess property, it must respond to the Notice of Availability within 30 days and then submit a formal request for the property to be transferred within 60 days from the date the notice expires. Agencies are required to pay fair market value to acquire excess property, although there are a number of circumstances under which an exception to this requirement may be approved.[12]

Public Benefit Conveyance

If no federal agency wants an unneeded property, it is declared "surplus" and made available to state and local governments, and nonprofits.[13] These entities may have surplus property transferred to them for a discount of up to 100% of fair market value, provided they use the property for a public benefit.[14] This type of transfer is called a public benefit conveyance, and to qualify, the property must be used for one of the following purposes:

- Homeless services
- Corrections
- Law enforcement
- Public health

- Drug rehabilitation
- Education
- Parks and recreation
- Seaport facilities
- Wildlife conservation
- Highways
- Emergency Management Response
- Historic monuments
- Public airports
- Housing

Each public benefit category has a federal agency, called a sponsor, that oversees conveyances for that purpose. Generally, sponsoring agencies have expertise in the policy areas they sponsor. The Federal Aviation Administration, for example, is the sponsoring agency for public airport conveyances.[15]

Pursuant to Title V of the McKinney-Vento Homeless Assistance Act, surplus properties must be made available for serving the homeless before being made available for other public benefit uses.[16] The Department of Housing and Urban Development (HUD) is responsible for reviewing surplus property to determine if it is suitable for homeless use. If a property is determined to be unsuitable for homeless use, then it becomes available for other public uses at that time. If HUD determines a surplus property is suitable, however, it publishes a notice to that effect in the *Federal Register*. State and local governments, and nonprofits, are given 60 days to notify the sponsoring agency, the Department of Health and Human Services (HHS), that they are interested in using the property for serving the homeless.[17] If HHS receives an expression of interest within the 60-day window, the property may not be made available for any other purpose until action on the request is complete. If no interest is expressed, then the property becomes available for other public benefit uses.[18] GSA advertises its availability by contacting state and local officials and known nonprofits with an interest in the property. GSA may also post notices in city halls, state capitols, and other appropriate locations.[19] The sponsoring agency is generally responsible for distributing, reviewing, and approving applications; conveying the property to the recipient; and monitoring the use of the property after it has been transferred, although GSA assists some agencies with these duties.[20] If the recipient of a conveyed property fails to use the property as agreed—by building a retail center on property conveyed for a public park, for example—then the property may revert back to the federal government.

Negotiated Sale

Surplus property that is not disposed of through the public benefit conveyance process may be sold to state and local governments at fair market value.[21] In essence, state and local governments are given the right of first refusal—they are allowed an opportunity to purchase surplus property before the property is offered for sale to the general public. Federal real property regulations permit negotiated sales when "a public benefit, which would not be realized from a competitive sale, will result from the negotiated sale."[22] The regulations do not specify what types of activities would qualify, but GSA guidance notes that a state or local government can use property "according to its own redevelopment needs," including economic development.[23]

Public Sale

Surplus properties that are still available after screening for public benefit conveyance and negotiated sale may be offered for public sale. The property is advertised in local newspapers, regional or national publications, and the U.S. Real Estate Sales list, and may also be found on GSA's website.[24] The appraised value of a property is used as a guideline for initial pricing, and properties are sold through sealed bids, physical auctions, and Internet auctions.[25]

Real Property Disposal at USPS and DOD

DOD and USPS are two of the three largest federal landholding agencies, as measured by owned square feet. DOD is the largest, with more than 1.7 billion square feet of owned space in its inventory, while USPS is the third largest with 197 million square feet of owned space.[26] Both DOD and USPS have independent statutory authority to dispose of unneeded real property, although the scope of that authority differs. While USPS has been given autonomy in disposing of all of its properties, DOD's disposal authorities are more limited and more complicated. The remainder of this section discusses the disposal process at each agency.

U.S. Postal Service[27]

Congress has given USPS independent statutory authority to dispose of its real estate as it deems proper.[28] USPS may

> acquire, in any lawful manner, such personal or real property, or any interest therein, as it deems necessary or convenient in the transaction of its business; to hold, maintain, sell, lease, or otherwise dispose of such property or any interest therein; and to provide services in connection therewith and charges therefor.[29]

Allowing USPS to make decisions over its real estate and property holdings has been viewed as integral to the concept of the USPS as encapsulated in the Postal Reorganization Act (PRA).[30] This 1970 statute replaced the Post Office Department (an appropriations-dependent agency) with the U.S. Postal Service (a financially self-supporting "independent establishment of the executive branch."[31] The PRA assigned USPS the "general duty" to "maintain an efficient system of collection, sorting, and delivery of the mail nationwide."[32] In order to carry out this obligation, Congress provided USPS with a number of powers to generate revenue and control its operational costs, including the authority to "determine the need for post offices, postal and training facilities and equipment, and ... provide such offices, facilities, and equipment as it determines are needed."[33] This authority over real property has helped USPS respond to shifts in population by expanding its presence in areas where the number of people and businesses was growing, and scaling back USPS's operational footprint in places where population was decreasing. This authority over its property and facilities also permits USPS to alter its logistical (mail-moving) network to accommodate mail volume changes and technological developments in mail processing.[34]

Disposal of Postal Properties

USPS policy is to dispose of excess real property under the terms and conditions that provide the greatest value to the Postal Service. Disposition may be by sale, exchange, outlease, sublease, or by other means determined to be in the best interest of the Postal Service.[35] In addition, USPS has employed private real estate companies to sell some of its excess or unneeded properties.[36] The agency also has auctioned some of its properties, including the Chicago Main Post Office, a 14- story property of 3 million square feet.[37]

Both federal law and the USPS's rules prescribe a post office closure process, which takes at least 120 days.[38] The USPS must notify members of the public who may be affected by the closure, and hold a 60-day comment period prior to closing a post office. Should the USPS decide to close a post office, the public has 30 days to appeal the decision to the Postal Regulatory Commission (PRC).[39] Sixty days after USPS has made a closure decision, the agency may shut down a post office, regardless of the outcome of the PRC's review.[40] Federal statute does not require USPS to take public comment when it disposes of properties that are not post offices, such as properties utilized as office space.

Department of Defense[41]

DOD comprises the Office of the Secretary of Defense (which includes all defense agencies and field activities); the Joint Chiefs of Staff; the Combatant Commands (such as Central Command, Northern Command, and Strategic Command); and the military departments of the Army, Navy, and Air Force. All real property is placed under the jurisdiction of one of the military departments.

Individual defense facilities fall under the immediate responsibility of a local installation military officer who could be referred to as the garrison commander, the base wing commander, the base commander, or the station commander, depending on the service administering the site.

The following sections will first describe the identification and disposal of military real property under routine practice, then the special procedures that were authorized under the Defense Base Closure and Realignment Act of 1990,[42] as amended. The latter process is commonly known as a Base Realignment and Closure (BRAC) round.

Routine Disposal of Real Property

The officers entrusted with administration of a defense site are required to periodically review the current and anticipated utilization of its land and facilities. A change in military strategy or doctrine, mission, operations, military equipment, or units based at a given facility could similarly change the need for site infrastructure. If the officer in charge determines that certain real property is no longer needed, he or she forwards a recommendation to "excess" the property up the appropriate chain of command. The final authority for declaring real property to be excess rests with the Secretary of the relevant military department, though the responsibility for managing real property inventory is usually delegated to an Assistant Secretary.

Once defense property is identified as excess, the administering military service submits a report to GSA. Other defense organizations, both active and reserve, may request that all or part of it be transferred to them. GSA then screens the property for potential use by other federal agencies. If no agency expresses interest within a reasonable period, the property is considered surplus, and GSA then directs and supervises the disposal process discussed elsewhere in this report.

Congress has imposed several statutory disposal restrictions and reporting requirements on DOD and codified them in a number of sections within Title 10 (Armed Forces) of the United States Code. Included among them are

- 10 U.S.C. 2662, which requires that, for real property with an estimated value in excess of $750,000, the Secretary concerned report to the House and Senate Committees on Armed Services any (1) transfer of real property to another federal agency or another military department or to a State, or (2) report of excess real property to a disposal agency (such as GSA), wait 30 days (14 days if the report is made by electronic medium) before undertaking the transaction, and report again within 30 days of entering into the transaction;
- 10 U.S.C. 2694a, a section that authorizes a Secretary to convey to a State, one of its political subdivisions, or a nonprofit organization any surplus real property under his jurisdiction that is suitable for conservation purposes, has been made available for a public benefit conveyance,[43] and is not subject to a pending request for transfer to another federal agency, after notification of the relevant congressional committees and waiting 21 days;
- 10 U.S.C. 2696, which both allows military department secretaries to transfer real property under their jurisdiction between themselves without compensation and requires the GSA Administrator to screen all defense real property for further federal use before a Secretary conveys it under any provision of law enacted after December 31, 1997, though there are some exceptions and special provisions for land intended for use as a correctional facility.

BRAC: Special Temporary Disposal Authorities and Procedures

The cessation of operations and closing of a major military installation will often entail a significant impact on the economy and social structure of the communities in its vicinity. Therefore, successive Secretaries of Defense have found over the past several decades that a number of statutory and political constraints have rendered the process, and prospects, of significantly reducing the defense real property "footprint" problematic.

Since the waning days of the Cold War, Congress has from time to time granted special temporary authority to the Secretary of Defense to carry out wholesale reviews of domestic defense real property with the intention of evaluating and reducing the inventory deemed excess to defense needs and surplus to federal requirements. All told, five defense real property disposal series have thus far been authorized. Though created under different laws, each series has become commonly referred to as a Base Realignment and Closure, or BRAC, round.[44] The most recent authorization for a BRAC round expired on April 15, 2006, so any new effort would have to be authorized by the enactment of a new provision of law.

While BRAC rounds have not seen an alteration of the general three-step process (identification, screening, and disposal), the temporary statutes creating them have added a number of features that enhanced oversight of DOD, offered assistance to the communities affected, and increased the transparency of the mechanism by which garrisons are reconfigured and installations are realigned to new missions or shuttered. In addition, many of the provisions of the McKinneyVento Homeless Assistance Act (42 U.S.C. 11301 et seq.) and the National Environmental Policy Act (42 U.S.C. § 4321 et seq.) have been applied to property closed under BRAC much as they do to other federal surplus property.

The differences between the normal real property disposal process carried out by GSA and that initiated by DOD during a BRAC round can be summarized around their three general phases, identification, screening, and disposal. The details following pertain to the processes used during the most recent (2005) BRAC round carried out under the FY2002 reauthorization of the Defense Base Closure and Realignment Act of 1990.

Identification of Property under BRAC

During the 2005 BRAC round, the Secretary of Defense was required to draw up and submit to Congress a "force-structure plan," based on an assessment by the Secretary of the probable threats to the national security during the 20-year period beginning with FY2005, the probable end-strength levels and major military force units (including land force divisions, carrier and other major combatant vessels, air wings, and other comparable units) needed to meet these threats, and the anticipated levels of funding that will be available for national defense purposes during such period[45] and a comprehensive world-wide inventory of military installations for each military department, with specifications of the number and type of facilities in the active and reserve forces of each military department.[46]

DOD was required in the statute to use a set of eight "final selection criteria," divided into "military value criteria" and "other criteria," in making recommendations for closure or realignment. Roughly paraphrased, the four military value criteria for each installation centered on (1) mission capabilities and readiness, (2) availability of facilities, (3) capacity to absorb mobilization surges, and (4) the cost of operations. Other criteria included (1) timing of potential savings, (2) economic impact on surrounding communities, (3) ability of communities to support the installation, and (4) environmental impact. The statute required that only these criteria be used and that priority consideration be given to the military value criteria.[47]

Once identified by DOD, the Secretary of Defense submitted his list of recommended closures or realignments to an independent nine-member commission for further consideration. Appointed by the President, with congressional input, and confirmed by the Senate, the commission and its staff were required to hold public hearings on the Secretary's recommendations. During its deliberations, the statute allowed the commission to add a new installation to the closure or realignment lists or increase the extent of a realignment only if it determined "that the Secretary deviated substantially from the force-structure plan and final criteria" specified earlier and concluded that its amendment was consistent with both. The statute required the commission to submit its own report to the President by a date certain.

Approval and Implementation of Closures and Realignments

After receiving the commission's report, the President was given a finite period of time to submit to Congress and the commission his approval or disapproval of the commission's recommendations. If he disapproved, in whole or in part, the commission's list of recommendations, he was instructed to state his reasons for doing so. The commission then had approximately one month in which to revise and resubmit its list. A second disapproval would have halted the process.[48]

Once having received the President's certification of approval, Congress gave itself a period of 45 days during which it could pass a joint resolution of disapproval using an expedited procedure laid out in the governing statute. If enacted, such a joint resolution would prevent the Secretary of Defense from carrying out any recommended closure or realignment.[49] If not thereby halted, the statute required the Secretary of Defense to initiate all closures and realignments within two years and complete them within six years of the date that the President recorded his approval.

Disposal of Real Property

The statute provided the Secretary of Defense with authority to offer economic adjustment assistance to any community near a closing or realigning military installation and community planning assistance to communities whose local installations absorb functions during the process.[50] This assistance has usually been channeled through "local redevelopment authorities" (LRA) nominated by the affected communities and so designated by the Secretary of Defense. It is to these LRAs that title to surplus property is usually conveyed.

The base closure acts have also provided other special authorities. Their provisions have directed the GSA Administrator to delegate to the Secretary of Defense his or her authorities to utilize excess properties and dispose of surplus properties for installations being closed or realigned. In addition to being able to dispose of surplus property at below market value through public benefit conveyances, the Secretary has been able to do the same if the LRA has agreed to apply proceeds from the sale or lease of property to the economic redevelopment of the site.

While DOD retains responsibility for the remediation of environmental contamination at former defense sites, the statute places no time limit on either remediation or on the conveyance of the property from the federal government.

Environmental Requirements and Historic Preservation

The transfer of surplus federal property may be subject to an array of environmental requirements intended to protect human health and safety, natural resources, and cultural resources.[51] Which requirements may apply to the transfer of a property would depend upon the site-specific conditions, such as the presence of wastes, contamination, and other potential hazards. For example, federal facilities that manage hazardous wastes or underground storage tanks are subject to closure requirements similar to private industrial facilities. If contamination is present, remediation may be required to prevent potentially harmful exposures subsequent to transfer. Some federal facilities also may contain more unique hazards, such as unexploded ordnance on DOD installations or radiological wastes from the past production of nuclear weapons at Department of Energy (DOE) facilities. Federal facilities not involved in industrial operations still may contain hazardous substances from other sources that could present challenges for transfer and reuse, such as asbestos or lead-based paint in buildings. In addition to human health and safety hazards, the potential impacts of a transfer on certain natural or cultural resources (such as historic buildings) also must be assessed. How such resources would be protected by the recipient of a federal property subsequent to transfer may be a potential issue.

The time and resources necessary for compliance with environmental and historical requirements may vary considerably among individual properties depending on applicability. The process of determining which federal requirements may apply and how compliance must be demonstrated is sometimes referred to as the environmental review process (or environmental and historical review). Actions necessary to complete the review process are generally integrated into the broader due diligence process established in federal regulation, during which the landholding agency would be required to assess and determine various details about the property, such as[52]

- any past activities or present conditions at the site that could pose a human health or safety hazard—the existence of mold hazards, radon hazards, asbestos-containing materials, or lead-based paint in any building; whether pesticides have been applied in the management of the property; or whether past activities at the site resulted in the release of hazardous substances that must be remediated;
- the property's location—in a federally designated floodplain, wetland, or coastal zone; or in an area that contains federally threatened or endangered species; and
- the property's historical significance—a site, buildings or fixtures on the site that are historically, architecturally, or culturally significant.

For each criterion, at a minimum, the landholding agency would be required to evaluate the property to determine whether or not such conditions or issues exist. Depending on that evaluation, the agency may be required to comply with certain environmental laws, regulations, or executive orders before they can make a final decision regarding the disposition of the property. Certain federal requirements may apply specifically because the property disposition would involve a transfer from federal ownership. That is, the disposition may be subject to certain requirements that generally would not apply (or could apply differently) to property transfers between nonfederal agencies or private entities. The principal federal statutes that govern the environmental review process, identification and remediation of hazardous substances, and historic preservation are outlined below, followed by a summary of the requirements of each statute. Other federal and state laws also may apply to a property transfer depending on the site-specific conditions.

- The National Environmental Protection Act (NEPA; 42 U.S.C. §§4321 et seq.). Under NEPA, federal agencies must consider the environmental impacts of an action before making a final decision about that action. With regard to surplus property disposal, the responsible federal agency would be required to identify impacts associated with both reporting the property as excess and disposal of the property, but not necessarily its future development that would not constitute a federal action itself.
- The Comprehensive Environmental Response, Compensation, and Liability Act of 1980 (CERCLA; 42 U.S.C. §§9601 et seq.). Section 120(h) of CERCLA generally requires federal agencies to clean up contaminated federal property prior to transferring the property out of federal ownership, unless assurances are provided that the cleanup will be carried out subsequent to transfer and certain conditions are satisfied. To ensure compliance with CERCLA, a federal agency would be required to certify whether or not hazardous substance activity took place during the period of federal ownership and whether, as a result, hazardous substances were released that may warrant remediation.
- The National Historic Preservation Act (NHPA; 16 U.S.C. §§470 et seq.). Section 106 of NHPA requires any federal agency with jurisdiction over a proposed federal undertaking to take into account the effect that the undertaking will have on any district, site, building, structure, or object that is included in or eligible for inclusion in the National Register of Historic Places (i.e., a property significant in American history, architecture, archaeology, engineering, or culture).

Some level of compliance with NEPA and CERCLA generally would be required for all federal agency actions related to the closure and disposal of federal surplus property, at least to document whether there would be any significant environmental impacts with respect to NEPA and whether hazardous substances may be present with respect to CERCLA. Compliance with NHPA would be required if the property being disposed is included or eligible for inclusion in the National Register or if its disposal would affect such a property. Within the framework of documenting any environmental impacts associated with the property disposal, under NEPA, the responsible agency would incorporate information on how compliance with CERCLA would be demonstrated and whether compliance with any other laws, such as NHPA, would be required.

The National Environmental Policy Act[53]

Signed into law in 1970, NEPA has been interpreted as having two primary goals—to ensure that federal agencies consider the environmental impacts of their actions *before* a final decision is made about the action, and to require those agencies to inform the public of those impacts. As a procedural statute, NEPA is intended to inform a federal agency's decision-making process, but does not require that agency to elevate environmental concerns above others.

Regulations implementing NEPA were promulgated by the Council on Environmental Quality (CEQ).[54] Those regulations identify actions subject to NEPA to include those over which a federal agency[55] has some control or responsibility.[56] For example, NEPA may apply to federal agency decisions on the adoption of agency plans and the approval of specific projects. That is, any planning decision or approval that must be made by the landholding agency regarding surplus property disposal may be subject to some level of review under NEPA.

For non-BRAC properties, agency actions subject to NEPA generally include those related to decisions regarding the (1) closure of the facility and reporting it as excess; and (2) disposition of the property.[57] After it accepts a property for disposal from another federal agency, GSA takes responsibility for completing the NEPA process for any subsequent disposal-related activities. However, the landholding agency would be required to complete any necessary NEPA review for actions that pertain to its decision to report the property as excess.

While multiple actions related to surplus property disposal may be subject to NEPA, the analysis required to document compliance is usually limited. The most extensive level of analysis, the preparation of an environmental impact statement (EIS), is rarely required for surplus property disposal. An EIS is required for actions that will significantly affect the quality of the human environment.[58] Among other requirements, it must identify and analyze any impacts of the proposal and identify all reasonable alternatives to the proposal, as well as the impacts of those alternatives. With the exception of federal actions undertaken as part of the BRAC process, federal real property disposal rarely involves significant environmental impacts.

For federal real estate transactions, significant impacts generally occur (i.e., the preparation of an EIS may be required) when the action is likely to involve major new construction. That may be the case when a federal agency is buying property for development, but not generally when disposing of a property. While a property transferred from federal ownership may be further developed, the landholding agency is not required to determine how a potential buyer may use the property before making a decision to dispose of it. Often property disposal involves the disposition of a property that has already been developed. Implementing the BRAC process, however, involves the closure of one military property and the potential expansion of another. As a result, decisions implementing the BRAC process have been those most likely to require the preparation of an EIS.

Regardless of whether an EIS would be required, agencies are obligated to identify the potential impacts of the disposition to ensure that it would not have significant impacts. If the impact of the proposed disposition is uncertain, an agency may ensure compliance with NEPA by preparing an environmental assessment (EA). The result would be either a decision to prepare an EIS or to issue a finding of no significant impacts (FONSI).[59] NEPA compliance may also be documented as part of a categorical exclusion (CATEX) determination.[60] A CATEX is applied to actions that individual agencies have determined, based on their experiences with similar actions in the past, have no individually or cumulatively significant effect on the environment.[61] CEQ allows an action to be processed as a CATEX as long as it involves no extraordinary circumstances that could result in significant impacts.

Each federal agency's procedures to implement NEPA[62] explicitly list actions likely to be approved as a CE or, under certain conditions, an EA. For example GSA's NEPA procedures identify specific actions that can demonstrate compliance with NEPA by completing a "CATEX checklist."[63] That checklist is used to ensure that a given action would involve no extraordinary circumstances that would result in significant environmental impacts. Included among such action, GSA explicitly identifies property disposal actions undertaken for another federal agency, where that agency has already documented compliance with applicable legal requirements such as NEPA, NHPA, and CERCLA; and disposal of real property required by public law wherein Congress has not specifically exempted the action from the requirements of NEPA.[64]

A determination that the disposal of surplus federal property would result in no significant impacts, under NEPA, is not equivalent to determining that the disposition would result in no regulated impacts. For example, if a federal property is listed on the National Register of Historic Places, the impact of its disposition may be deemed insignificant, but only if there are certain restrictions placed on the future use or development of the property. Within the context of ensuring compliance with NEPA, the landholding agency may be required to identify measures necessary to ensure future protection of the resource. In this instance, the requirement to protect that resource could originate with the NHPA (or any other applicable law intended to protect cultural, archaeological, or historical resources), not NEPA. Still, the NEPA compliance process may not be complete until decisions have been made regarding how the landholding agency will ensure compliance with those other applicable laws.

As noted above, one of NEPA's primary goals is to inform the public of the environmental impacts of a proposed action. CEQ regulations implementing NEPA specify public involvement requirements that apply primarily to actions that require an EIS. However, individual agencies have determined that public participation may also be appropriate in the preparation of an EA/FONSI or when determining whether the action may involve some exceptional circumstances that would prevent the application of a CATEX. Each agency has discretion in determining the level and kind of public participation required for such actions. For surplus property disposal, the level of public participation will likely depend on the nature of property itself and the potential public interest in that property's potential closure and disposition.

There may be public opposition to the closure and disposition of surplus federal property. The reasons for such opposition will be unique to that property. However, opposition could arise if there is public concern that future development of the land would no longer be subject to certain federal requirements. For example, after the property transfers from federal ownership (e.g., to a local or state agency or to a private developer), the impacts of future development would generally not be subject to federal agency review or public comment under NEPA or NHPA. Another example of such a law is the Archeological and Historical Preservation Act (AHPA). It requires federal agencies to identify and recover data from archeological sites threatened by their actions. Since a nonfederal land owner would not be required to take such action, members of the public may want the landholding agency to ensure that the property has been adequately surveyed to identify archeological sites or to make the sale conditional on a buyer agreeing to implement certain actions if archeological sites are later discovered.

The Comprehensive Environmental Response, Compensation, and Liability Act[65]

The Comprehensive Environmental Response, Compensation, and Liability Act (CERCLA) is the principal federal statute that addresses releases of hazardous substances into the environment on both federal and nonfederal lands.[66] Section 120(h) of CERCLA generally requires the United States to clean up contaminated federal property prior to transferring the property out of federal ownership.[67] The policy premise of this provision is that the United States should assume full responsibility for the cleanup of contamination caused by federal activities, and not shift the burden of that responsibility to the recipient merely as a consequence of acquiring the property.

Section 120(h) applies to all contaminated federal property declared surplus to the needs of the federal government. The agency with administrative jurisdiction over a surplus federal property generally is responsible for performing and paying for the cleanup of contamination to fulfill the financial liability of the United States. In some cases, the recipient may voluntarily agree to pay for the cleanup of a contaminated surplus federal property in exchange for a discounted purchase price to acquire the property, or other conditions of ownership that the recipient may desire.

As is the case with federal facilities that remain in federal ownership, funds available for the cleanup of surplus federal properties are subject to the availability of appropriations to the federal agencies that administer those properties. For example, the Department of Defense (DOD) performs and pays for the cleanup of surplus federal property on military installations closed under a consolidated Base Realignment and Closure (BRAC) round out of funds appropriated to the DOD Base Closure Account. Federal facilities generally are not eligible for cleanup funds appropriated to the Environmental Protection Agency (EPA) under the Superfund program, which addresses nonfederal sites elevated for priority federal attention. However, EPA oversees the cleanup of federal facilities through the Superfund program in conjunction with the states, in a manner similar to the enforcement of cleanup liability at nonfederal sites. At federal facilities, the administering federal agency serves as the responsible party on behalf of the United States.

Section 120(h) of CERCLA does not bind the United States to cleaning up a surplus federal property for any one particular land use. As a result, the reuse of a property is negotiated between the administering federal agency and the recipient of the property. Disagreements over reuse can arise if the recipient intends to use the property for a purpose that would necessitate a level of cleanup that the federal agency may consider too costly, relative to available appropriations to fund the cleanup. The capabilities of cleanup technologies also could constrain the reuse of a surplus federal property, if it would be impractical to achieve a level of cleanup that would be needed to make the property suitable for a use that the recipient may desire.

Continuing Liability of the United States

Consistent with the policy premise of Section 120(h) of CERCLA and retroactive liability under Section 107[68] of the statute, the United States remains responsible for contamination found not to have been sufficiently remediated after the property is transferred out of federal ownership. Section 120(h)(3) requires the continuing liability of the United States to be specified through a "covenant" incorporated into the deed transferring the property out of federal ownership.[69] The covenant must warrant that all remedial actions necessary to protect human health and the environment have been taken before the date of transfer, and that the United States shall conduct any additional remedial actions found to be necessary after the date of transfer. A clause also must be included in the deed granting the United States access to the property to perform cleanup actions for which it may be responsible.

In practice, the contents of a deed can place certain limitations on the continuing responsibility of the United States. A deed to a transferred federal property typically warrants cleanup only to a level suitable for the land use negotiated prior to transfer. In some cases, a deed may include a restriction prohibiting certain uses that would be considered unsuitable relative to the level of cleanup performed by the United States. Under such deed restrictions, the United States typically assumes responsibility for additional cleanup only to the extent that more work is found to be needed to make the originally agreed-upon use suitable.

If the new owner later decides to use the property for a different purpose, the new owner typically must assume responsibility for the additional cleanup costs to make the property suitable for the desired purpose. In some instances, a deed may prohibit certain land uses even if the new owner is willing to pay the cleanup costs. For example, a deed to a decommissioned military training range may prohibit residential or other land uses because of limitations on cleanup technologies to detect and remove unexploded ordnance. Cleanup capabilities may be constrained especially when ordnance is located beneath the surface, or concealed on the surface by dense vegetation.

Transfer of Uncontaminated Parcels

Some surplus federal properties may contain a mix of contaminated and uncontaminated parcels of land. Although the clean parcels may be ready for reuse, the requirement to clean up the contaminated parcels under Section 120(h) of CERCLA prior to transfer could delay the conveyance of the property as a whole. To address such situations, the 102nd Congress enacted the Community Environmental Response Facilitation Act (CERFA; P.L. 102-426) in 1992. This law amended Section 120(h) by adding a new subsection (4) that authorizes the transfer of uncontaminated parcels on a surplus federal property while cleanup continues on the contaminated parcels.[70] This parcel-by-parcel approach is intended to avoid potential delays in the transfer of "clean" surplus federal lands for reuse, especially such lands on closed military installations where economic redevelopment is desired to replace lost jobs. In the event that previously unknown contamination is later discovered after transfer out of federal ownership, Section 120(h)(4)(D) requires that a deed to an uncontaminated parcel still include a covenant warranting that the United States shall conduct cleanup actions that may become necessary to address contamination attributed to past federal activities.[71]

Early Transfer of Contaminated Parcels

The cleanup of a contaminated parcel may take several years or more, depending on the type and level of contamination, technical feasibility of cleanup actions, and availability of appropriations to pay for the cleanup. In such situations, the requirement to complete cleanup prior to transfer out of federal ownership could result in delaying the transfer. Enacted in the 104th Congress, Section 334 of the National Defense Authorization Act for FY1997 (P.L. 104-201) amended Section 120(h)(3) of CERCLA to add a new subsection (C) that allows the transfer of a contaminated parcel on a surplus federal property before cleanup is complete, if certain conditions are satisfied.[72] Although Congress enacted this amendment in annual defense authorization legislation, this authority applies to any surplus federal property administered by any federal agency, not just surplus U.S. military property.

Section 120(h)(3)(C) specifically authorizes a deferral of the cleanup covenant to allow the transfer of title to a contaminated parcel on a surplus federal property before cleanup is complete. Federal agencies often refer to this deferral of the covenant as an "early" transfer, although the statute does not use this term. The deed to a contaminated property transferred out of federal ownership must contain assurances that the cleanup still will be carried out after the property leaves federal ownership. The federal agency responsible for the performance of the cleanup also must identify the funding needed to carry out the cleanup in its annual budget requests.

The deed also must restrict the use of the property to purposes that would be protective of human health and environment, while the cleanup proceeds. For example, at the time of transfer, a property may be suitable for industrial use because the risks of exposure to contamination may be within an acceptable range, whereas other land uses that would result in potentially harmful exposure would be restricted until the property is cleaned up sufficiently for that purpose. Once cleanup is complete, the United States remains obligated to provide a covenant at that time, warranting that all necessary actions to protect human health and the environment have been taken to make the property suitable for its intended, eventual use.

The early transfer of a contaminated surplus federal property that EPA has designated on the National Priorities List (NPL) for cleanup purposes is subject to the concurrence of the Administrator of EPA and the governor of the state in which the facility is located. The early transfer of a contaminated surplus federal property that is not listed on the NPL still requires the concurrence of the governor of the state in which the facility is located, but not EPA. Federal agencies proposing an early transfer also must provide the public at least 30 days advance notice and an opportunity to comment on the proposed transfer before it is executed.

National Historic Preservation Act[73]

When federal property is sold, a review under the National Historic Preservation Act[74] (NHPA) may be required to determine whether the action will adversely affect historic properties and how to mitigate those effects. Courts describe NHPA as a "stop, look, and listen" statute that directs an agency to consider the effects of its action on historic sites, but does not require an agency to stop a project that would harm that property.[75] Instead, NHPA requires an agency to make an informed determination following a decision making process that is known as a Section 106 review.[76]

Federal agencies conduct a Section 106 review when their actions, known as *undertakings*, may affect a historic property. An *undertaking* is defined as "a project, activity, or program funded in whole or in part under the direct or indirect jurisdiction of a Federal agency."[77] The Section 106 process begins before federal funding is provided or a federal license issued.[78] Starting a Section 106 review early in the project development process ensures that agencies consider "a broad range of alternatives" during the planning process.[79]

When a federal agency finds an action is an undertaking, its first step is to identify the parties required to be involved in the decision making process, who are known as *consulting* parties. NHPA regulations define who must be invited as a consulting party,[80] including the State Historic Preservation Officer (SHPO), the Tribal Historic Preservation Officer (THPO), local and tribal officials, and, if the federal undertaking involves issuing a permit, the applicant. Other *interested* parties may participate, such as historic associations and general members of the public, but do not have the same standing in the decision making process as the consulting parties.[81]

Next, the agency identifies the area of potential effects (APE), defined as "the geographic area or areas within which an undertaking may directly or indirectly cause alterations in the character or use of historic properties."[82] At this stage, the action agency, with the consulting parties, identifies historic properties that may be affected. Historic properties are defined as those listed or eligible for listing in the National Register of Historic Places.[83] If no historic properties are within the APE, the Section106 process concludes.

When historic properties are found within the APE, the agency will coordinate with the consulting parties to determine whether the undertaking will adversely affect the property. If no adverse effects are found, the Section 106 process ends. The undertaking does not have to touch a historic property physically for an agency to find an adverse effect, as the NHPA regulations state that the agency must consider both direct and indirect effects of the project,[84] as well as reasonably foreseeable effects that may occur later in time or at some distance, or are cumulative.[85] Accordingly, NHPA would apply not only to selling federally owned historic buildings but may also apply when the sale of a non-historic building would adversely affect historic properties. For example, if the sale of a non-historic federal building could change the character of a historic area, that might be considered an adverse effect and would require further analysis.

If adverse effects on historic properties are found, NHPA does not require the agency to reject the undertaking. Instead, the agency is required to compile adequate documentation of its adverse effects findings, make the documentation available to the public, and provide an opportunity for comment.[86] An additional consulting party may be invited at this stage—the Advisory Council on Historic Places (ACHP or the Council).[87] The agency, with the cooperation of the consulting parties, shall "develop and evaluate alternatives or modifications to the undertaking that could avoid, minimize, or mitigate adverse effects on historic properties."[88] When the parties agree on avoidance and/or mitigation of the adverse effects, the agency and the SHPO/THPO will enter into a binding agreement known as a Memorandum of Agreement (MOA),[89] and consulting parties are invited to concur.[90] Completion of a MOA concludes the Section 106 process.

If the parties cannot reach an agreement on the adverse effects, the agency, the SHPO/THPO, or the Council may terminate the Section 106 process.[91] The terminating party must notify the others in writing of the basis for ending consultation, and the ACHP will provide the opportunity for the parties (including itself) and the public to comment. However, termination of the Section 106 process does not mean that the project must also be terminated. If the agency decides to continue the undertaking, the agency must document its rationale and demonstrate that it considered the comments of the Council.[92] The agency must give a copy of this document to the consulting parties and make it available to the public.[93] Then, the agency may advance its project despite any harm to historic properties, taking any mitigation measures it chooses.

End Notes

[1] Federal Real Property Council, FY2013 Federal Real Property Report: An Overview of the U.S. Federal Government's Real Property Assets, August 2014, p. 1.

[2] U.S. Government Accountability Office, Federal Real Property: Progress Made in Reducing Unneeded Property, but VA Needs Better Information to Make Further Reductions, GAO-08-939, September 2008, p. 9.

[3] U.S. Government Accountability Office, Federal Real Property: Excess and Underutilized Property is an Ongoing Problem, GAO-06-248, February 2006, p. 3. For more information, see CRS Report R40476, Base Realignment and Closure (BRAC): Transfer and Disposal of Military Property, by R. Chuck Mason.

[4] Federal Real Property Council, FY2013 Federal Real Property Report: An Overview of the U.S. Federal Government's Real Property Assets, August 2014, p. 15.

[5] This section was written by Garrett Hatch, Specialist in American National Government, x7-7822.

[6] 40 U.S.C. §101 et. seq. Land reserved for national forest or national park purposes, and Bureau of Land Management properties, are not covered by these disposal rules. Other legislation that governs federal agency real property disposal includes the National Historic Preservation Act (16 U.S.C. §470 et. seq.), which establishes guidelines for agency disposition of historic properties, and the Stewart B. McKinney Homeless Assistance Act (42 U.S.C. §11411), which requires agencies to make surplus real property available first for homeless use before making it available for other purposes. In addition, Executive Order 13327, signed in 2004 by President George W. Bush, established (1) Senior Real Property Officers (SRPOs) at 24 of the largest landholding agencies to monitor and manage their agencies' real property, (2) a Federal Real Property Council, comprised of SRPOs, to evaluate agency real property policies and practices, and (3) the Federal Real Property Profile, a database with information on agency real property holdings, including disposition data.

[7] The Department of Defense has the authority to dispose of unneeded real property that is subject to the Base Realignment and Closure (BRAC) process, but GSA disposes of non-BRAC real property. The U.S. Postal Service has the authority to dispose of all of its real property. The Departments of State, Veterans Affairs, Education, Health and Human Services, the Interior, and Agriculture also have the authority to dispose of some unneeded real property, although the scope of that authority varies widely.

[8] 40 U.S.C. §102.

[9] U.S. General Services Administration, Customer Guide to Real Property Disposal, p. 17, at http://www.missionumatilla.com/documents/historical_data/HD0013_PropertyDisposalClosureGuide_GSA.pdf.

[10] The Office of Real Property Utilization and Disposal website address is https://extportal.pbs.gsa.gov/ ResourceCenter/viewproperties.do?noticetype=1.

[11] Only the 24 federal agencies are required to report their real property data annually to the FRPP, although other agencies have the option of reporting. The agencies that are required to report are the Departments of Agriculture, Commerce, Defense, Education, Energy, Health and Human Services, Homeland Security, Housing and Urban Development, the Interior, Justice, Labor, State, Transportation, the Treasury, and Veterans Affairs; Environmental Protection Agency; General Services Administration; National Aeronautics and Space Administration; National Science Foundation; Nuclear Regulatory Commission; Office of Personnel Management; Small Business Administration; Social Security Administration; and United States Agency for International Development.

[12] See 41 C.F.R. §102-75.1275; 41 C.F.R. §§102-75.190-102-75.225; and 40 U.S.C. §522. When an agency is required to pay fair market value for a property, the government does not realize any new revenue since the funds are being transferred from another federal agency.

[13] 40 U.S.C. §102.

[14] 40 U.S.C. §549.

[15] 40 U.S.C. §550. The agencies that sponsor conveyances are the Departments of Education (education), Health and Human Services (public health, homeless services), the Interior (parks and recreation, historic monuments, wildlife conservation), Justice (correctional), Transportation (port facility), Housing and Urban Development (housing), Justice (law

enforcement), Homeland Security (emergency management response), and the Federal Aviation Authority (public airports).

[16] 42 U.S.C. 11411.

[17] 41 C.F.R. §102-75.1200.

[18] Conveyances, other than McKinney Act transfers, are at the discretion of the agency and are not required by statute.

[19] U.S. General Services Administration, Surplus Real Property Available for Public Use: Notification Procedure, GSA website, at http://www.gsa.gov/Portal/gsa/ep/contentView.do?contentType=GSA_BASIC&contentId=20146.

[20] U.S. General Services Administration, Customer Guide to Real Property, p. 25. The General Services Administration is responsible for deeding, conveyance, and compliance monitoring of correctional, law enforcement, and emergency management conveyances, and for just deeding and conveyance of properties to be used for historic monuments, or public airports.

[21] 41 C.F.R. §102-75.880(d); 40 U.S.C. §545.

[22] Ibid.

[23] U.S. General Services Administration, Office of Real Property Utilization and Disposal, "How to Acquire Federal Property," at https://extportal.pbs.gsa.gov/ResourceCenter/content/acquireFedProp.do.

[24] General Services Administration, Office of Real Property Utilization and Disposal, Current Sales webpage, at https://extportal.pbs.gsa.gov/ResourceCenter/PRHomePage/ loadPR HomePage.do?type=full.

[25] General Services Administration, Customer Guide to Real Property Disposal, p. 27.

[26] Federal Real Property Council, FY2013 Federal Real Property Report: An Overview of the U.S. Federal Government's Real Property Assets, August 2014, p. 1.

[27] This section was prepared by Garrett Hatch, Specialist in American National Government.

[28] Thus, for example, Congress exempted USPS from the federal property disposition statutes (40 U.S.C. §101).

[29] 39 U.S.C. 401(5).

[30] P.L. 91-375; 84 Stat. 725 (39 U.S.C. §101 et seq.)

[31] 39 U.S.C. 201. With the PRA, Congress relinquished a great deal of control over USPS's operations as that control had proven problematic. Congressional directives often inhibited the Post Office Department from controlling its operating costs and increasing its prices.

[32] 39 U.S.C. §403(b).

[33] 39 U.S.C. §404(a)(13).

[34] Over the past century, the proportion of mail sorted by postal workers has greatly declined with the advent of machinery that can read the addresses on letters and parcels and sort them according to their destination.

[35] U.S. Postal Service, U.S. Postal Service Facilities Guide to Real Property Acquisitions and Related Services, Handbook RE-1, October 2008, p. 15, at https://about.usps.com/handbooks/re1.pdf.

[36] For example, see http://www.uspspropertiesforsale.com/.

[37] Staff, "Let the Bidding Begin," Chicago Tribune, August 27, 2009, at http://articles.chicagotribune.com/2009-08-27/ news/0908260669_1_condos-minimum-bid-requirement-real-estate.

[38] 39 U.S.C. 404(d); and 39 C.F.R. 241, "Post Office Organization and Administration: Establishment, Classification, and Discontinuance," at 76 F.R. 41413-41424, July 14, 2011

[39] 39 U.S.C. 404(d) sets the PRC's role in the appeals process.

[40] For a more detailed description of the post office closure process, see CRS Report R41950, The U.S. Postal Service: Common Questions About Post Office Closures, by Kevin R. Kosar, pp. 6-7.

[41] This section was prepared by Daniel H. Else, Specialist in National Defense.

[42] See 10 U.S.C. 2687 note.

[43] State and local governments and certain nonprofit organizations may qualify for a public benefits conveyance of surplus public property at reduced or no cost for a number of specified uses.

[44] So-called BRAC rounds were carried out in 1988, 1991, 1993, 1995, and 2005. The 1988 round was authorized by Defense Authorization Amendments and Base Closure and Realignment Act (P.L. 100-526, §1, 102 Stat. 2623). The 1991, 1993, and 1995 rounds were authorized by the Defense Base Closure and Realignment Act of 1990 (part A of Title XXIX of P.L. 101-510). Both acts were codified in 10 U.S.C. 2687 note. The 2005 round was created in a reauthorization of the 1990 law enacted in the National Defense Authorization Act for Fiscal Year 2002 (P.L. 107-107, Division A, Title X, Subtitle E, §1048(d)(2), Division B, Title XXVIII, Subtitle C, §2821(b), Title XXX, §§3001-3007, 115 Stat. 1227, 1312, 1342).

[45] Defense Base Closure and Realignment Act of 1990, as amended, Section 2912(a)(1)(A).

[46] Ibid., Section 2912(a)(1)(B).

[47] Ibid., Section 2913.

[48] The President has not yet disapproved any commission's recommendation list.

[49] For more information on joint resolutions, see CRS Report 98-728, Bills, Resolutions, Nominations, and Treaties: Characteristics, Requirements, and Uses, by Richard S. Beth and CRS Report 98-706, Bills and Resolutions: Examples of How Each Kind Is Used, by Richard S. Beth. Though resolutions have been introduced in one chamber or the other during every BRAC round, none has survived its initial floor vote.

[50] The Secretary's Office of Economic Adjustment has served as the principal organization through which such assistance has been offered.

[51] An overview of environmental requirements that may apply to the transfer of surplus federal property is available in the General Services Administration (GSA) "Environmental Framework for Real Property Disposal" at http://propertydisposal.gsa.gov/ EnvironmentalInfo.

[52] GSA regulations identifying the information required from federal departments and agencies for property declared excess to their needs are codified at 41 C.F.R. Part 102-75, Subpart B. The criteria that must be evaluated under these regulations before GSA will accept a property for disposal also are identified in GSA's "Excess Real Property Checklist" (available at http://propertydisposal.gsa.gov/FAA). The checklist is a supplement to its "Standard Form 118, Report of Excess Real Property." When the Postal Service, DOD, and DOD agencies dispose of their own excess real property, each agency is required to evaluate similar criteria.

[53] This section was prepared by Linda Luther, Analyst in Environmental Policy.

[54] 40 C.F.R. Parts 1500-1508.

[55] "Federal agencies" are defined at 40 C.F.R. §1508.12 to include all agencies of the federal government, but not Congress, the Judiciary, or the President.

[56] 40 C.F.R. §1508.18.

[57] Congress, not individual military agencies, identifies military bases that are subject to closure as part of the BRAC process. As a result, base closure decisions are not subject to NEPA. However, the military agency responsible for the base closure may have a certain degree of

discretion in implementing the closure, as well as the action that must be taken to realign the activities at the closing base with another facility. Actions taken to implement the base closure are subject to NEPA.

[58] As required at 42 U.S.C. §4322(2)(C). In accordance with the CEQ regulations, the significance of a proposal's impacts are determined on a case-by-case basis depending on the context and intensity of those impacts (see 40 C.F.R. §1508.27). Also, CEQ defines the "human environment" to include the natural and physical environment and the relationship of people with that environment (see 40 C.F.R. §1508.13).

[59] See 40 C.F.R. §§1501.3 and 1508.9.

[60] CATEXs are referred to as such because they are actions that are categorically excluded from the requirement to prepare an EIS or EA.

[61] See 40 C.F.R. §1508.4

[62] Each federal agency was required to adopt the CEQ regulations implementing NEPA and to supplement them with procedures necessary to implement NEPA that are relevant to the action undertaken by that agency. GSA, USPS, and DOD, as well as each of agency within DOD, have done so.

[63] See the "PBS National Environmental Policy Act NEPA Desk Guide," October 1999, Section 5.4 Checklist CATEXs. The NEPA Desk Guide is available at http://www.gsa.gov/nepadeskguide.

[64] See the GSA's NEPA Desk Guide, Sections 5.4(c) and (g).

[65] This section was prepared by David M. Bearden, Specialist in Environmental Policy.

[66] 42 U.S.C. §9601 et seq. For a broader discussion of CERCLA, see CRS Report R41039, Comprehensive Environmental Response, Compensation, and Liability Act: A Summary of Superfund Cleanup Authorities and Related Provisions of the Act, by David M. Bearden.

[67] 42 U.S.C. §9620(h).

[68] 42 U.S.C. §9607.

[69] 42 U.S.C. §9620(h)(3).

[70] 42 U.S.C. §9620(h)(4).

[71] 42 U.S.C. §9620(h)(4)(D).

[72] 42 U.S.C. §9620(h)(3)(C).

[73] This section was prepared by Kristina Alexander, Legislative Attorney.

[74] P.L. 89-665, 80 Stat. 915; 16 U.S.C. §§470 et seq.

[75] See Safeguarding the Historic Hanscom Area's Irreplaceable Resources, Inc. v. Federal Aviation Administration, 651 F.3d 202, 214 (1st Cir. 2011); Business and Residents Alliance of East Harlem v. Jackson, 430 F.3d 584, 591 (2d Cir. 2005); Muckleshoot Indian Tribe v. U.S. Forest Service, 177 F.3d 800, 805 (9th Cir. 1999); Illinois Commerce Commission v. Interstate Commerce Commission, 848 F.2d 1246, 1261 (D.C. Cir. 1988).

[76] It is named after the section within the public law enacting NHPA, P.L. 89-665, §106, but is codified at 16 U.S.C. §470f.

[77] 16 U.S.C. §470w(7); 36 C.F.R. §800.16(y).

[78] 16 U.S.C. §470f.

[79] 36 C.F.R. §800.1(c).

[80] 36 C.F.R. §800.2(a)(4).

[81] For example, the agency is not required to confer with interested parties, unlike consulting parties, on key issues such as resolving any adverse effects, as discussed later in this section.

[82] 36 C.F.R. §800.16(d).

[83] 36 C.F.R. §800.4.

[84] 36 C.F.R. §800.16(d).

[85] 36 C.F.R. §800.5(a)(1).

[86] 36 C.F.R. §800.6(a)(4).

[87] The ACHP is an independent federal agency. It is required to be invited to participate in developing an MOA under three circumstances: if a National Historic Landmark will be adversely affected (36 C.F.R. §800.6(a)(1)); if a programmatic agreement affecting multiple agency undertakings is being prepared (36 C.F.R. §800.6(a)(1)); or if the parties fail to come to terms on a MOA (36 C.F.R. §800.6(b)(1)(v)).

[88] 36 C.F.R. §800.6(a).

[89] 36 C.F.R. §800.6(c)(1).

[90] 36 C.F.R. §800.6(c)(3).

[91] 36 C.F.R. §800.7.

[92] 36 C.F.R. §800.7(c)(4).

[93] 36 C.F.R. §800.7(c)(4).

INDEX

D

E

F

G

H

I

J

L

M

N

O

P

R

S